PREACHING THE GOSPEL OF JOHN

John F. O'Grady

Paulist Press
New York/Mahwah, NJ

The scripture quotations contained herein are from the author's own translation. Used by permission.

Poetry verses on page 4 are taken from "God's Grandeur" by Gerard Manley Hopkins, Nicholson and Lee, eds., *The Oxford Book of English Mystical Verse,* 1917: and from "Talk" by Yevgeny Yevtushenko, copyright © by Robin Milner-Gulland and the Estate of Peter Levi, 1962.

Cover and book design by Sharyn Banks

Cover photo from Church of the Good Shepherd, New York, NY, by Michael Kerrigan, CSP.

Library of Congress Cataloging-in-Publication Data

O'Grady, John F.
    Preaching the Gospel of John / John F. O'Grady.
        p. cm.
    ISBN 978-0-8091-4619-2 (alk. paper)
1. Bible. N.T. John—Homiletical use. 2. Catholic Church. Lectionary for Mass (U.S.)
3. Catholic preaching. I. Title.
    BS2615.55.O47 2009
    226.5′06—dc22

                                                                    2009018480

Published by Paulist Press
997 Macarthur Boulevard
Mahwah, New Jersey 07430

www.paulistpress.com

Printed and bound in the
United States of America

Contents

Preface vii

I. THE WORD OF GOD AND THE BIBLE
A. The Word of God: Foundation for Preaching 3

B. Biblical Hermeneutics 10

II. PREACHING AND THE PREACHER
A. The Preacher and the Word of God 23

B. The Homily 32

III. THE GOSPEL OF JOHN
A. The Theology and the Community of the
Gospel of John...39

B. Faith and Love: Foundations of the Community 49

C. The Jews in the Gospel of John 66

IV. THE GOSPEL OF JOHN IN THE LECTIONARY
Third Sunday of Advent B.......................................71

Christmas Mass During the Day 73

Third Sunday of Lent A 76

Third Sunday of Lent B 79

Fourth Sunday of Lent A 82

Fourth Sunday of Lent B 85

Fifth Sunday of Lent A...87

Fifth Sunday of Lent B..89

Fifth Sunday of Lent C..92

Holy Thursday...94

Good Friday 97

Contents

Easter Sunday 100

Second Sunday of Easter A-B-C 102

Third Sunday of Easter C 105

Fourth Sunday of Easter A-B-C................................108

Fifth Sunday of Easter A 112

Fifth Sunday of Easter B 115

Fifth Sunday of Easter C 117

Sixth Sunday of Easter A-C 119

Sixth Sunday of Easter B..122

Seventh Sunday of Easter A-B-C 124

Pentecost 128

Trinity Sunday A 131

Trinity Sunday C 134

Corpus Christi A 136

Second Sunday of the Year A 139

Second Sunday of the Year B 141

Second Sunday of the Year C 143

Seventeenth Sunday of the Year B 145

Eighteenth Sunday of the Year B 148

Nineteenth Sunday of the Year B 151

Twentieth Sunday of the Year B.................................154

Twenty-First Sunday of the Year B 156

Feast of Christ the King B 159

To the Memory of My Brother
Edward James O'Grady, 1930–2008,
whose love, compassion, kindness, and encouragement
are deeply missed by all who knew him and loved him.

Preface

For more than thirty-five years, I have studied and loved the Gospel of John. My doctoral thesis in scripture dealt with both the individual and the community. I have taught this gospel in every institution with which I have ever been associated, in particular the Pontifical Biblical Institute in Rome. I have written two small books on this gospel, as well as a number of articles and book reviews, and have thoroughly enjoyed preaching it in churches throughout the United States.

Even with many years of study, I continue to find verses in this gospel that I have never seen before. As I read the lectionary selections, I continue to see relationships that have previously escaped my observation. I return repeatedly to this gospel and see it again for the first time.

Over the years, many priests have complained to me how difficult it is to preach on this gospel, especially the sixth chapter, which occurs in the second lectionary cycle several weeks in a row. As a result, many do not like this gospel. In my great humility, I told them I had no trouble preaching so many weeks in a row on one chapter. They replied, "Well, write something to help us!" Such was the origin of this book.

I enjoy preaching and love to open up the Word of God to anyone who will listen. I would like think a bit of the poet exists within me. I also know I preach well. But like everything I have and do, the quality of my preaching depends on what I have been given by others.

In elementary school, my mother paid ten cents a week for the first four years of my education and twenty-five cents a week for the last four years for me to have private elocution lessons. My teachers were Sister Servants of the Immaculate Heart of Mary from Immaculata, Pennsylvania. I remain forever indebted to them.

My seminary professors, especially those at the Pontifical Biblical Institute, continued my education in this gospel. Nor could I ever forget my good friend and professor, Rev. Raymond Brown, SS (1928–1998), who even after his death continues to give me guidance through his many works on Johannine literature. When finishing my doctorate in scripture, I was invited to become a New Testament Fellow of Columbia University and for many years traveled from Albany to New York every Friday during the school year. Raymond Brown and Louis Martin were also members as were several other Johannine scholars (e.g., Ernst Käsemann and Moody Smith) who came as visitors. I kept my mouth closed and learned from them all. The one exception was the discussions on the identity of the Beloved Disciple. At the time, Father Brown was writing his book on *The Community of the Beloved Disciple*, and I had come to similar conclusions independently. Thirty years ago, I was pleased to receive the approval of such an outstanding scholar as Father Brown.

With good teachers in elocution and in scripture, especially those who taught me the Gospel of John, I believe I have become a good preacher on this gospel, and I offer to those who are interested the fruit of my many years of preaching about it.

Anyone who listens to me preach can detect a formula that I always use: text, context, context of congregation, response. First, I deal with the section from the lectionary. Then I place this text in its own context within the book from which it came, or within the historical period. Then I relate the meaning of the text to the context of the particular congregation and, finally, propose an expected response from the listeners. In the opening chapters, I explain this formula. Occasionally, as I present the sections from the lectionary, I will include an outline using this formula. I do not do it with every reading since so much depends on the context of the congregation on any particular day.

Many years ago, I wrote a weekly column for the Albany diocesan paper on the Sunday readings. I had some of these columns in my files, and my good friend Debbie Rossiter put them on a disk to help me in writing this book. I am indebted to her for her great kindness to me in many ways.

My mother (1900–77) gave me the opportunity to develop elocution skills. The Most Rev. Edwin B. Broderick, Bishop of Albany (1916–2006), sent me to the Pontifical Biblical Institute and encouraged me in every way to obtain a doctorate in scripture even though I was not at first interested in doing such a thing. He and my mother knew each other and enjoyed each other's company. Now they are both gone, but the influence they had on me continues.

Finally, my oldest brother Edward (1930–2008) always encouraged me personally and professionally, as priest, teacher, and writer. Both my mother and brother often enjoyed the company of Bishop Broderick. I believe that they continue to enjoy each other's company in the everlasting kingdom of God and of Jesus Christ.

Feast of St. Ignatius Loyola
July 31, 2008
Miami Shores, Florida

I.

THE WORD
OF GOD AND
THE BIBLE

A. The Word of God: Foundation for Preaching

Old clichés never seem to die. Catholics were never forbidden to read the Bible, but the medieval monasteries did chain their Bibles. This was not to discourage people from reading the Bible but to keep them from stealing it. Before the printing press existed, the Bible was hand-copied and of great value. No wonder monasteries and churches chained their Bibles. Other historical circumstances, however, did discourage Catholics from reading the Bible. During and after the Reformation, when Protestants had translated the Bible into the vernacular with their own interpretations, the Catholic Church became fearful that loyal Catholics would misinterpret the Bible and fall into what was considered the heresy of Protestantism.

In the United States, the Catholic Church began as an immigrant church with many people coming to this country with little or no formal education. The clergy were the educated ones, and they would not only read the Bible but would give a careful and accurate interpretation to their flocks. The people had their rituals, their prayers and sacraments, and these sacraments expressed the presence of Jesus, and these sufficed. To enhance their Catholic faith, the church encouraged devotions to Mary and the saints and the use of sacramentals such as holy water and holy pictures. With such devotional aids, along with a full sacramental system, the Bible was not emphasized.

Preaching most often concerned doctrine rather than using the Bible as the foundation for preaching. Priests preached sermons rather than homilies. In the Protestant tradition without a sacramental system, the Bible became the heart and soul of worship. No wonder Catholics would always say that their Protestant friends knew the Bible and they did not. With the changes over the last forty years, Protestants are becoming more sacramental, using many of the symbols and rituals of the Catholic tradition, and Catholics are becoming more interested and conversant with the Bible. Preachers moved from sermons to homilies. For both Catholics and Protestants, the Bible remains always the Word of God in the words of people.

WORDS

Some words divide: *black and white, rich and poor.* Some words unite: *sister, brother, friend.* Some words are sad: *pain, suffering,* and some words are happy: *joy, party, celebration.* Some words cut and some words heal. Some words are great and some words are small. The poet speaks the great words: *fire, love, kiss, sky, earth,* and *water.* The great words enter into the very depth of reality and pull up something that can lead to an appreciation and love of life.

> The world is charged with the grandeur of God.
>   It will flame out, like shining from shook foil;
>   It gathers to a greatness like the ooze of oil
> Crushed....

✦

> How sharply our children will be ashamed
> taking at last their vengeance for these horrors
> remembering how is so strange a time
> common integrity could look like courage.

World, charged, grandeur, God, greatness, generations—each word is a "great word" used powerfully by the pen of the poet Gerard Manley Hopkins. "Great words" uplift, enliven, celebrate, and soothe. In the hands of the poets, they transform. The poet Yevgeny Yevtushenko has also chosen some of the great words: *children, vengeance, horrors, integrity,* and *courage.* Each word brings to the human understanding something of the meaning of life. The primordial words reflect the human spirit. They bring about the unity of flesh and spirit, transcendence and perception, the abstract and the historical. They bring the reality they express, transferring a transcendent moment into human existence. The great words bring knowledge with the hope of love.

trans cadent dynamism (Rahner)

To the poet belongs the word but not to the poet alone. Poets speak the great words in powerful concentration. Others speak the powerful words but not as powerfully as the poet. The poet lives in transcendence just as other artists but in a different mode. Not everyone can participate in the visual or graphic arts or the beauty of sound or movement. However, everyone speaks words, everyone communicates and unites with others, and everyone speaks the great words at least on some occasions.

Reality longs to be known and loved. The poet who speaks the great words knows reality and life and some of life's hidden meaning. The poet conveys that meaning in a way that others can understand and then possibly love. Primordial words, the great words, function as a sacrament of what being human means.

The transcendent, the other, becomes imminent and those who *knowledge* hear the words are introduced into an ever-deeper sense of life. Knowledge and love make everyone appear to be infinite. No limit exists on what one can know. The genius still learns more. The person who teeters on the moronic can also learn more. No one can ever say, "I have learned enough" or "I have learned all that there is." Knowledge is a gift that makes a person appear to be without limits.

The same is true for love. An individual can never limit love, but *love* can always love more or love more deeply. Human love has no evident limits. The person can always increase those who are loved and love those who are part of life with a never-ending depth.

The poet knows the depth of knowledge and fashions some of that depth in the choice of the primordial words. With the knowledge that comes from the communicated words, the poet knows the possibility and actuality of love. Only someone who loves life and all that life means can choose the right words to convey the understanding of life— that in itself intensifies the love of life.

In the Jewish and Christian tradition, God speaks the Great Word: God is present in human history and God loves the human race. The knowledge and love needed by all humans become capsulized in words and experiences. In ancient times, whether God loved the human race remained a question. People were ambivalent. They wondered and came to differing conclusions. To assure them that the gods and goddesses loved them, they developed intricate rituals, hoping to placate what was often thought to be angry divinities. Israel and its faith changed this human misperception. God spoke in all of creation and through the mouth of the chosen prophets, and the Word of God expressed God's love.

THE WORD OF GOD

The Word of God lives, moves, and creates. All creation has its origins in the Word of God. People hear the Word, recognize it as coming from God, listen to it, and follow it. God spoke as recorded in Genesis and the world was formed from chaos. "God said, 'let there be light' and there was light. God saw how good the light was" (Gen 1:3–4). The Word of God goes forth and will not return until it has completed its task.

> For just as from the heavens the rain and snow come
>> down
> And do not return there till they have watered the earth
> Making it fertile and fruitful
> Giving seed to him who sows and bread to him who eats,
> So shall my Word be that goes forth from my mouth;
> It shall not return to me void, but shall do my will,
> Achieving the end for which I sent it. (Isa 55:10–11)

With the advent of Judaism, the one God of Abraham, Isaac and Jacob, Sarah, Rebecca, Rachel, and Leah established a covenant. This God of the fathers and mothers would be their God and they would be God's people: a chosen race, a royal priesthood, a people set apart (Exod 19:6). God always was present in creation. With Judaism, creation came into being by the very Word of God (Gen 1). Throughout the history of Israel, different individuals heard this one Word of God, made it their own, and preached this Word to others.

When he had his religious experience, Moses asked God: "What is your name?" (Exod 3). God replied by not replying: *Eyah asher eyah*. Hebrew has no system of tenses as does English. The principal tenses

6

are action completed and action not completed. Often in the past, these Hebrew words were translated as: "I am who I am." But they can also be translated as: "I will be who I will be." The latter makes more sense. God would not reveal the sacred name for knowing a person's name gives too much information. The people of Israel will discover who God is in their own history as God revealed through words and experiences.

During the period of the prophets, the Word of God frequently came to individuals with the imperative to both live the Word and preach the Word. For many, the Word was both salvation and judgment but in fact the Word brought only salvation. The failure to listen to the Word and live according to it brought the judgment of condemnation. God spoke a Word of creation and of judgment based on how people responded.

In the Exodus experience God entered into a covenant (*Berith*) with the Israelites. In the past, people interpreted this covenant as a reciprocal contract. God would remain faithful if people would remain faithful. In fact, even when the people did not remain faithful, God never changed. God remained the God of the people of Israel. God manifested the virtues of compassion, kindness, mercy, and fidelity in the presence of the contrary part and actions of the holy people of Israel. Repeatedly, God offered a covenant, an unconditional covenant of love and pardon. Again and again, people refused to listen but God never changed. The people of Israel remain always God's holy people.

Prophets heard the Word of God and proclaimed it. They were not interested in the future but were concerned with the present. They pointed out the presence or absence of God in their own times and among their own people. They were the ancient poets entrusted with the great Word of God that they spoke to all who would listen.

> The Word of the Lord came to me thus: Before I formed you in the womb, I knew you; before you were born I dedicated you, a prophet to the nations I appointed you. (Jer 1:4–5)

> He said to me, "eat what is before you; eat this scroll, then go speak to the house of Israel." So I opened my mouth and he gave me the scroll to eat…and it was sweet as honey in

my mouth. He said "Son of Man go now to the house of Israel and speak my Word to them." (Ezek 3:1–4)

For while gentle silence enveloped all things and night in its swift course was half gone, your all powerful Word leaped from heaven, from the royal throne. (Wis 18: 14–15)

JESUS, THE WORD OF GOD

Creation speaks the Word of God, the prophets spoke the Word of God, the Word leaped from heaven, and for Christians the Lord Jesus *is* the Word of God. "In the beginning was the Word and the Word was with God and the Word was God" (John 1:1).

Jesus was the Word of God made flesh and became incarnate. Jesus not only spoke the Word of God but lived as God's Word, offering knowledge and the love of God that he alone could do. Through Jesus, the unity between God and humanity was accomplished. Through Jesus, God communicated to people the Word of God. Through Jesus as God's Word, people learned to love God more deeply just as God loved the human race through Jesus. The Word of God now exists in a person, Jesus of Nazareth. Jesus is the great Word of God for Jesus speaks the one great Word: God loves all creation with a special love for people. In Jesus, God has given everything to people: "He who did not spare his own Son, but handed him over for us all, how will he not give us everything else along with him?" (Rom 8:32).

The Word of God enlightens people. People learn. Through this Word, God enters into a relationship with the human race. The Word of God unveils God, making the relationship with people possible. Certainly, this same Word exists in creation for people to hear. People can listen to the Word of God just by being alive. However, in a special way the Word of God exists in Judaism and Christianity. The offer of a relationship, personal, intrinsic, and transcendent in creation, becomes public, extrinsic, and categorical in salvation history.

The Word of God given to Moses and to the prophets and fulfilled in Jesus helped people in their relationship to God. Now the record of people hearing and responding to the Word of God in faith remains permanently recorded in the Bible. People still need to hear the Word of God personally and intrinsically, but they also can hear this Word in the history of Israel and in the history of Jesus and the early church.

In every instance, the Word of God became an event. Something happened and people changed. The Word accomplished what it set out to do. The presence of God becomes real in the Word spoken to Israel and the Word spoken and lived by Jesus of Nazareth. Many shared in the working out of God's Word in human history but none as powerfully as Jesus.

Historically, the Word of God varied in intensity and efficacy. Certainly all heard and spoke the Word of God as recorded in the Bible. But not all heard and spoke this Word with the same concentration.

> In times past God spoke in fragmentary and varied ways to our Fathers through the prophets. In this final age God has spoken to us through His son whom he has made heir of all things and through whom he has first created the universe.
> (Heb 1:1–2)

Each person who heard the Word contributed to the understanding of God and the offer of a relationship making Israel God's holy people. In Jesus, the Word of God incarnate, God has spoken definitively and has accomplished the perfection of this offer of a relationship, for in Jesus the offer and acceptance took place in the same person. As the record of the religious experience of Israel and of Jesus and his earliest followers, the Bible speaks the Word of God today to anyone who will listen. Like the Word of old, the Bible accomplishes what it offers. The one who hears the Word of God in the Bible becomes the subject on whom the Bible works its power. The one who studies the Bible as an object becomes transformed into the one affected by the Bible. The subject becomes the object. The Word of God continues its transforming effect and exercises its power. God has entrusted the Word to the church and to the preachers. They, like poets, speak the great words, and the one powerful Word of God has its effects. Both preachers and congregations are changed. The Word accomplishes what it sets out to do. The awesome responsibility of relating the Word of God to believers lies with those chosen to preach. They need to understand both the Bible and their congregations. They need to be poets.

B. Biblical Hermeneutics

The contemporary preacher must feel confused with the vast array of contemporary approaches to scripture. Long gone are the days when the preacher struggled to deal with the literal sense and then make some kind of application. Any quick perusal of summaries on contemporary hermeneutics almost creates a sense of despair. Even the word *hermeneutics* often only adds to the confusion. With so many voices, often disparate and even contradictory, who can make any sense of what all these "so called experts" are saying? Some would like to return to giving sermons and leave the labyrinth of scripture studies to the experts. But scripture remains the Word of God, and that alone forces the diligent preacher to try to sort out the various contemporary approaches to the eternal Word of God as recorded in the Bible. Preaching homilies demands some understanding of contemporary biblical studies.

HERMES AND HERMENEUTICS

Hermeneutics is not a new word even if for some it continues to cloud the issue. Hermes is the Greek messenger god who becomes Mercury in Latin mythology. Hermes knows something and delivers his knowledge or message to an audience. He knows the subject, knows the recipient, and knows how to get from one to the other. Every good preacher follows the example of Hermes. Like Mercury, preachers have wings on their feet that swiftly help the movement from knowledge in one person to knowledge in another. Hermeneutics is the art of delivering a message to a particular audience. It involves knowing the message, knowing how to deliver it, and knowing the audience.

EXTREMES IN INTERPRETATION

Two extremes characterize contemporary biblical interpretation: fundamentalism and good human-interest stories. The former considers everything the Bible records to have actually happened and the words *style* spoken to have come from the proposed speakers. Verbal inspiration lies at the foundation of fundamentalism. God, through the Holy Spirit, inspired the sacred author to write each word as personally dictated by God. Moreover, all of the events of the Bible actually occurred as recorded even if opposing evidence seems formidable. Otherwise, God would not be telling the truth and such a thought would be blasphemous.

Even though there were no walls around Jericho and perhaps it was not even inhabited when Joshua attacked the ancient city, the walls actually fell down at the blast of the trumpets. The Bible says so. People can feel secure in what they read since it comes from the very mouth of God. Anyone who would question the historicity of such events lacks true faith.

Jesus was born in Bethlehem. Magi came from the East bearing gifts. He went with his parents to Egypt because Herod wished to kill him. The events narrated actually happened, even if Matthew seems to base his story on the Old Testament paralleling the origins of Moses and responding to the demands on his Jewish/Christian and Gentile/Christian community.

Peter spoke in Aramaic at Pentecost and everyone understood Peter in his or her own native language. Even if contemporary scholarship shows that this story seems more like the reversal of the tower of Babel, it happened as presented.

Biblical fundamentalism has not been part of the Catholic tradition even if some Catholics, including preachers, seem to favor it. Since the 1943 encyclical *Divino Affflante Spiritu* of Pope Pius XII on scripture, Catholics have been encouraged to use all of the methods of historical criticism that negate a naive fundamentalism.

The other extreme views the Bible as a collection of wonderful *style* stories with little or no historical foundations. Just as Grimm's fairy tales continue to have merit as does Greek mythology, so the Bible can be used by contemporary people to gain some insights into human life. As a human document, the Bible contains errors in science, history, and geography as well as in psychology and sociology. It also offers poetry, prose, fables, legends, parables, wise sayings, edifying stories, and a host of other types of literature all geared to inspire the one who wishes to be inspired. The value is totally subjective, and the same truth can be found in a number of other literary works.

The Bible may truly contain errors in history or geography or science since it has its origins as a document of faith and not as a book with biographies or a history or science book. The Bible as the Word of God does contain some history and means more than just passing on good human-interest stories to edify simple people.

Needless to say, both extremes must be avoided in interpreting the Bible even if both have some truth. God does speak in the Bible, and the Bible does contain errors and many human-interest stories along with many exaggerations.

ADVOCACY HERMENEUTICS AND POSTMODERNISM

Between these two peaks in contemporary interpretation lies a vast valley within which most preachers can easily find themselves lost. Two approaches within this valley are usually rejected out-of-hand: advocacy interpretation and postmodernism. An advocacy interpretation uses the Bible to promote views held by the proponents. To advocacy exegetes, the stories of David and Jonathan clearly represent a homosexual relationship and so the Bible supports homosexual activity. Moses demanded that Pharaoh let his people go and so the Bible supports liberation theology. The Hebrew linguistic origin for the name Sarah is the same as the name Israel. Therefore, the Bible implicitly supports feminist theology that had previously been suppressed.

Although many will dismiss advocacy interpretation, no doubt the proponents of this approach at least ask questions that were not asked previously. A new viewpoint helps in understanding the Bible even if, for the most part, it seems to be reading too much into biblical quotations.

The other approach to the Bible usually dismissed centers on deconstructionism or postmodernism. The name most frequently associated with this interpretation is Jacques Derrida, a French literary critic. What scares people in this approach is the danger of extreme relativism. Critics describe postmodernism as the relativization of the

12

relative. The study of history, however, does relativize the present. History is like a vast river from which those who recorded human events took from the waters what they wanted and handed on to others what they saw of value. Different people from different times and cultures reach into the river and take what they want, and studying the different elements taken from the river of history does relativize any one record.

To the exegetes using this approach, no one book is absolute. The traditions about Abraham, Moses, and Israel are all created to suit a specific purpose. Even contradictory conclusions can result. The New Testament presents many images of Jesus, each offering something, but none offering everything. Even taken together, no one can develop a complete picture of Jesus and his ministry. All is colored by historical circumstances, and today all interpretations are colored by the interpreter.

Using only this approach can easily cause concern. But like the advocacy approach, postmodernism makes its contribution. The study of history does relativize any person, event, text, or even ritual. Religions and religious figures cannot be removed from their particular moment of history. The limitations necessarily become evident when someone in the twenty-first century absolutizes a person, event, saying, or ritual from centuries or even millennia ago. Postmodernism reminds interpreters to be sober and cautious in interpretation.

TEXT AND FORM CRITICISM

For the most part, other approaches to the interpretation of scripture have been readily accepted by most contemporary preachers even if they do not always understand them. Text criticism is easy enough: What were the original words and what did they mean etymologically? For some preachers, the constant new translations of the Bible into English annoy rather than help. Actually, the continual refining of the Hebrew and Greek text gives greater and greater accuracy in translations.

The Greek word *porneia* in Matthew 5:32 has been translated into English as unchastity, adultery, unlawful union, and fornication. Clearly, the diverse English words used in translation do not help when the entire verse states: "Everyone who divorces his wife except on the ground of *porneia* causes her to commit adultery and whoever marries a divorced woman commits adultery." Knowing the meaning of *porneia* has great importance for Christianity. Unfortunately, scholars differ on its meaning.

Since poetry and prose differ significantly, readers should know when they are reading what. The same is true for parables, stories, legends, and history. Most of the stories of the patriarchs are legends. Even some of the stories associated with Moses are legends, and the same might be true for David and Solomon. But the last three are also important figures in the history of Israel even if their stories have been retold in ways that make them larger in death than in life. Much of Job is poetry. The story of Jonah is a parable. For interpretation, knowing the type of literature involved helps the reader and the preacher to understand a text.

REDACTION CRITICISM

Redaction criticism concentrates on how and why any author wove together history, traditions, and stories to suit a particular audience. Each author had a particular theology and purpose attempting to respond to the faith needs of a particular group of people at a set moment in history. Redaction criticism helps the preacher first to understand from where a book came before trying to make this record of God's word applicable to the church today.

The second and third chapters of Genesis probably come from the court of David and deal with problems associated with court life as well as everyday life: the temptation to decide for oneself what is good or bad (the tree of good and evil) and the temptation to worship a false god (symbolized by the serpent). Ancient creation stories become joined to a theology of good and evil and the problems of the people of Israel at the time of David.

The Gospel of John comes from a community that differed, not in essentials, but in application of the Jesus tradition. The author was probably not one of the Twelve but an eyewitness from Jerusalem. He founded the community and gave it guidance and direction. While the founder lived, the community of the Fourth Gospel was more charismatic than structured.

The theology and historical circumstances of this gospel will help the preacher more clearly understand the meaning of the text and assist in relating the meaning of the text to a contemporary congregation.

NARRATIVE CRITICISM

Narrative interpretation concentrates on the story aspect of the Bible. While some may consider the historicity irrelevant, others accept some historical foundation but concentrate on the meaning. Whether or not Magi came from the East to recognize Jesus as the Messiah is a good story with a helpful lesson for Christians: Christianity is open to all, Jew and Gentile, and sometimes those least expected will be the first to belong. When the Magi became interracial in the Middle Ages, this was a good addition to a good story. All races belong as well as Gentiles and Jews. The leaders of the Jewish people fail to recognize Jesus as the Messiah while Gentiles offer gifts.

SOCIAL CRITICISM

Social criticism studies the text as reflecting and responding to the social and cultural setting from which it arose. When people today better understand the social and cultural milieu of the writings, they can have a better grasp of what the text meant to the original readers and then can make application to the present day.

Semitic society in the period of the Patriarchs, Judges, and Kings contributed to the composition of the books of the Old Testament. Trying to understand these texts today demands an understanding of these customs. Knowing the social convention of ascribing anonymous works to famous people helps to explain the many epistles attributed to Paul, even if most think some were written long after the death of Paul.

OTHER METHODS IN INTERPRETATION

Over the years other approaches to interpretation have arisen: historical criticism, rhetorical criticism, canonical criticism, reader/response criticism, transactive criticism, and so on. The concerned reader can seek further analysis in R. Brown's work, *An Introduction to the New Testament* (New York: Doubleday, 1997) or G. Montague, *Understanding the Bible* (New York: Paulist Press, 1997). But what can all this contribute practically to preaching the Word of God?

Some principles from biblical hermeneutics for the preacher:

1. Use a good English text in preparation, even if different from the prescribed lectionary.

2. Know the general background of the book from which the text is taken.

3. Relate the text under consideration to the theology of the author or book or community.

4. Recognize the value of the story: what the text meant to the original listeners or readers.

5. Avoid absolutizing any text or book of the Bible, and include the nonabsolutizing of the New Testament over the Old Testament.

Some principles for preaching the Word of God:

6. Know the context of the audience.

7. Relate numbers 1–5 to 6.

8. Offer some possible responses.

THE TEXT

The Revised Standard Version and the New Revised Standard Version Bibles are, in the opinion of most, the most accurate. Although the RSV contains much biblical English, "thou" and so on, it remains more faithful to the Hebrew and Greek texts than does the NRSV. A Catholic edition of the NRSV has the deuterocanonical books inserted within the Old Testament. The Revised New American Bible is also a good translation. The preacher will find it helpful to compare various translations. The Greek/English interlinear gives almost a word-for-word translation under the Greek text. This also can prove helpful when facing difficult texts.

KNOW THE BACKGROUND OF THE BOOK

The best way to learn this is to use a commentary. For example, Isaiah 1—39 can be understood only if the preacher knows something of the history of Israel in the eighth century before Christ. The Gospel of Mark makes sense when the preacher knows the circumstances of the Marcan community, most probably in Rome and clearly experiencing persecution. The Gospel of John becomes clearer when the community of the Beloved Disciple takes on its peculiar contours.

KNOW THE THEOLOGY OF THE BOOK

Following the aforementioned examples, Isaiah preaches both judgment and salvation with the emphasis on salvation. Judgment is what people bring upon themselves. Salvation is God's undeserved gift to the chosen people. Mark offers his community the example of a suffering Messiah to give hope for a suffering community. Just as the early followers (the Twelve and the disciples) had trouble with faith, so the community of Mark should not be surprised if people have trouble in believing. The theology of the Fourth Gospel emphasizes faith in Jesus and love of the brethren as primary.

THE VALUE OF THE STORY

Many times the student of the Bible can become so involved with interpretation that the story becomes lost. Each book of the Bible teases the mind into reflection. The story of Moses and the burning bush shows both the openness of Moses to God as well as God's interest in people. Sinai demonstrates both God's fidelity and people's fickleness. The story of the Magi encouraged Christianity to be open to all, especially the Gentiles. The shepherds in Luke show the concern of Jesus for all who live on the margins of society. The death of Jesus in the Fourth

Gospel shows how God is still present when bad things happen to good people, in death, and even in an unjust death by crucifixion.

DON'T ABSOLUTIZE ANYTHING

The Bible has many books from different periods. The Bible interprets itself. The historical books help interpret the prophetic books, and all should be influenced by the Wisdom literature.

The New Testament has four gospels, not one. Each presents something of value taken from the river that is the historical Jesus. Paul offers his interpretation of Jesus and his teachings. Other New Testament writings emphasize one or another part of the Jesus tradition. One gospel is not better than the others. One letter of Paul, usually Romans, is not the true dogmatic treatise of Pauline theology.

Finally, the New Testament makes sense only in the light of the Old Testament. Christians can never dismiss or even overlook the Word of God expressed in the full Bible. Christians need to understand the Old Testament as well as seek understanding of the New Testament.

RELATE NUMBERS 1–5 TO 6

The first five principles deal with text and context of the section of the Bible proclaimed. The stilling of the storm in Mark 4 fits into the general context of a community beset with the storms of persecution. Jesus calms the storm and then tells his disciples that they have no faith. In Mark, Jesus has power over all evil, even over the forces that lurk beneath the surface of the Sea of Galilee. If Jesus has power over this type of evil, he also has power over the evil of persecution. The disciples need to renew their faith and the storm will pass.

People today are still in the same boat. The boat is rocking, storm-tossed. Their faith is weak. Can God really be interested? Is Jesus really present to believers in times of danger? But with faith the storm passes.

Matthew in chapter 8 has the same story, but the background of this gospel and his theology differ. Matthew comes from a community of Jewish and Gentile Christians who recognize the need for organization for continuity. They know the church will be around for years to come and will continually experience problems and difficulties. The context for this story comes from following Jesus. Before Matthew narrates the story, three times he uses the word *follow* (8:19, 22, 23). Disciples follow Jesus into the boat, into the church. Jesus remains in the boat, in the church, and the boat experiences a storm. Immediately the disciples pray: "Save us, Lord." Before rebuking the storm, Jesus speaks to his disciples: "Why are you afraid, oh you of little faith?" Then he calms the storm.

Jesus never abandons his church. When the church faces the problems of living as people of faith, living with both Jewish and Gentile Christians causing all of the problems of trying to integrate two very different communities, they should pray to their Lord with confidence. Jesus does not immediately calm the storm but reminds them of their need to strengthen their faith. With prayer and faith renewed, the storm passes.

The contemporary parish often has to integrate different groups. Praying together and recognizing the need for a strengthening of each other's faith, help.

The reading for the first Sunday of Lent, Noah and the ark, deals with God's relationship to people and to creation and ends with a promise not to destroy the Earth again by flood. It almost seems that the author thinks God has gone too far in destroying creation and so God promises not to do it again. Goodness should not be destroyed because of the presence of evil.

The story falls within the first eleven chapters of Genesis that treat the struggle between good and evil. People bring evil upon themselves and God brings goodness. All of creation was good until people introduced evil and sin. In the end, goodness will win. The story of Noah contributes one story among many in these chapters of Genesis dealing with good and evil.

People always struggle with good and evil. True repentance, associated with Lent, demands an examination of how people are living. Repentance presupposes the presence of goodness in spite of evil and sin. God is good, creation is good, and people are good. People bring evil and sin upon themselves. In spite of the presence of evil and sin,

God will not destroy. As long as life perdures, repentance is possible. People can change and start again.

CONCLUSION

Hermeneutics involves both knowing the text and communicating. The preacher, by experience, also knows that good communication depends upon knowing the congregation. The context of any passage in scripture helps explain the meaning of the text, and the Bible itself helps explain the context of any book. The actual context of preacher and congregation also figures in effective communicating, and homilies conclude with some expected response.

Various approaches to the study of scripture help the preacher with the text and context of the text. The contemporary study of the many approaches to the Bible contributes immensely to the knowledge needed to understand the message to be communicated. Hermeneutics makes sense, especially since the various interpretations offer to the preacher another river from which he can take elements, moments, teachings that will suit the both the congregation and him as they sit together on the riverbank.

II.

PREACHING AND THE PREACHER

A. The Preacher and the Word of God

PREACHING

Preaching involves related and often disparate elements. Someone has to preach, and the content usually includes the Bible. When preaching at Mass, the context is liturgy and should always include the Bible. Preaching at the Eucharist differs considerably from a lecture or a conference or even a sermon, for example, at a retreat. Finally, the congregation should always be included in any effort to speak about the Word of God. A change of congregation, whether because of occasion or because of particular makeup, will often dictate not just what is said but how it is said. Homiletics becomes complicated when all of these elements of necessity must be interrelated.

THE PREACHER

The preacher will be effective to the extent that the one who proclaims God's Word has a self-image of one who has been entrusted with the Word of God. This differs considerably from the teacher, although often the element of teaching must be included. If the preacher is also an administrator, counselor, religious educator, financial planner—supposed to be an expert in marriage problems, family difficulties, personnel problems; interested in community matters; and involved with other Christian churches and interfaith dialogue—the role as preacher can frequently become lost in a myriad of other demands for time and commitment. Such, unfortunately, is the case for most pastors and preachers.

If the pastor as preacher, however, sees his role as primarily ministering the Word of God to members of the congregation, then some priority will help in deciding where to invest time and energy. Every individual has only so much psychic energy and time. With every organization and individual in a parish asking for a piece of the one who is supposed to be dedicated to preaching, priorities need to be set and some demands just have to be abandoned. No one can do everything. But how can the pastor as preacher so structure life to allow for adequate time for preaching and become more effective? The answer to the first question is deeply personal. Only the busy pastor can respond. Some helpful hints can help to respond to the second question.

Preachers should begin with themselves and examine their strong and weak points. On close examination they are the same: personality, knowledge, experience, and mechanics; voice, gestures, inflection, and so on. Some individuals have a personality that automatically supports the role of a preacher. Others have to overcome some personality characteristics to be a preacher. Knowledge of both Bible and congregation differs from preacher to preacher. Some have had the good fortune to study the Bible leisurely and also have had the opportunity to know many different congregations. Others have not.

Knowledge of scripture received in the seminary no longer suffices. The preacher needs additional study. The knowledge of one congregation may give experience of one type of audience, but experience of many congregations over a long period of time enriches the knowledge of the one who preaches and makes the person a more effective preacher. The one who has preached for thirty years has much more experience than the preacher who has just begun a ministry. Finally, the mechanics of preaching come easily to some but involve work and difficulty for others. This aspect of preaching is also deeply personal. Awareness of personal strengths and weaknesses is a beginning.

THEOLOGY OF THE PREACHER

If the primordial words are entrusted to the poet, the Word of God is entrusted to the priest/preacher. Certainly priests do not have an exclusive claim to the Word of God, but through ordination they accept the vocation to listen personally to the Word of God and to speak it to others. Priests minister to people through the Word of God.

The first responsibility to those ordained is to speak the Word of God to those entrusted to their care.

The Word of God belongs to the church. The church expresses this one Word in various degrees of intensity and concentration through its own life and through the life of its members. While the Word belongs to the whole church, priests fulfill their vocation precisely as ordained when they devote their ministry to the Word of God.

Some may object that such a limitation to ordained priests unfairly limits officially preaching the Word to ordained priests and excludes all others, including deacons. Actually, the Acts of the Apostles supports this opinion:

> The Twelve assembled the community of disciples and said, "It is not right for us to neglect the Word of God in order to wait on tables. Look around among your own number, brothers, for seven men acknowledged to be deeply spiritual and prudent. And we shall appoint them to this task. This will permit us to concentrate on prayer and the ministry of the Word." (Acts 6:2–4)

In the Acts of the Apostles, deacons have not been given the task to preach even if such is true in the contemporary church. Deacons historically assisted bishops in their pastoral activity that did not include preaching. The relationship of Word in preaching and Word in sacrament, especially the celebration of the Eucharist, gives to the priest a unique responsibility in preaching.

Traditionally, along with the ministry to the Word the priest also administers the sacraments. In fact the two ministries are one. The Word of God lives in the church in various degrees, and so in the celebration of the sacraments the priest proclaims the one Word of God for members of the church at times that are most critical for God's saving presence in an individual's life.

The one Word of God speaks to the individual at birth and death, and when one becomes conscious of death through sickness. This same Word promises the presence of the Spirit of God when an individual assumes the position of a committed Christian; when two people of faith commit themselves to each other in marriage; when an individual assumes a leadership role in the church; and in the midst of human failure and sin when the person of faith needs assurance from the Word of God that he or she is still beloved of God and the church. Finally, the one Word of God reaches its culmination when the priest proclaims the presence of Jesus as the incarnation of the Word of God in the celebration of the Eucharist as he says: "This is my body; this is my blood."

THE PRIEST AS POET

The true poet speaks the word from the heart. The priest who is most priestly also speaks the Word from the heart. But what if the Word does not always come from the heart of the priest? While the Word of God speaks to others through the priest, the Word of God is not limited to the priest. It accomplishes what it sets out to do. If nothing more, the Word of God humbles the priest, because he knows that like all other members of the church he remains a sinner throughout his entire life. He not only preaches the healing and merciful Word of God, but also hears it himself.

The priest speaks the great and primordial Word of God, a Word of love, mercy, forgiveness, compassion, kindness, and fidelity. In this sense the priest is always a poet even if many times he is less than an ideal poet. Just as the poet releases the primordial words and sets them free, so the priest releases the primordial Word of God and freely this one Word accomplishes the bringing of God to people and people to God.

Through his entire being, the priest speaks the Word of God in the church. He proclaims the one Word always in the church and of the church. Just as the Word cannot fail, so neither can the church even if the priest does not always live up to his high calling of being God's poet for others.

All that makes up the priest should proclaim the Word of God. But even if the priest sometimes fails the church does not. The church must proclaim God's Word with its very being. The priest does likewise with the presence of the grace of God. If the priest proclaims the Word of God in all that he is, then it is not only the great and primordial words that express the Word of God but also the small words. Much of the Old Testament is poetry. The Psalms immediately come to mind. Job is almost exclusively poetry, and many of the prophetic books are poetry. The New Testament contains hymns such as the prologue of the Gospel of John and the hymn in Philippians 2. Who could deny the poetry in the parable of the prodigal son, the priestly prayer of Jesus in John 17, and the hymn to love in 1 Corinthians 13? The Bible cherishes the great and primordial words and contains the small and useful words. They all serve the one Word of God.

The priest can call upon the poet so that the great and primordial words can become consecrated to the Word of God. The poet calls to the priest and reminds him that the great and primordial words express the richness of life and the loveliness of human existence. The poet asks the poetic question as he or she seeks to understand the transcendent. The priest responds to the poetic question by proclaiming that the great Word of God has entered into human history in Jesus.

Occasionally, the priest is a poet and the poet is a priest. God often works in serendipitous ways and the church, the world, and the people experience blessedness from God. Even when the priest is not a true poet, he speaks poetic words for he speaks the Word of God to others. Making the Word of God central to his life, the priest as preacher has the foundation to be the instrument of God's Word for others.

CONTENT: THE BIBLE

Homiletics begins with the Bible. God has spoken to the people of Israel, to Jesus, and through Jesus to his early followers. The Bible, as the record of this relationship between God and people, offers people today an opportunity to understand their own relationship to God by learning about the relationship between God and Israel and God and Jesus and his followers. The record of these religious experiences recorded in the Bible enables people today to deal with their own religious experience. Over more than a thousand years of history dealing with God and the human race, every possible experience with God and every possible reaction to God have been recorded in this one book. The Bible contains not only what happened to the Jews and to Jesus and his early followers, but also offers a good understanding of what it means to be human and how the religious dimension must figure in every human life. Even the very denial of the religious dimension so common today can find its correlation within the Bible. The Bible offers helpful hints for daily life and urges people to see how the religious dimension carries with it a better resolution to the vexing questions of life. The Bible always forms the fundamental content of preaching.

THE CONTEXT: LITURGY

Homiletics takes place within the context of liturgy, an expression of the faith of both preacher and congregation. People of faith pray together, led by the one who presides, who almost always also preaches. Liturgy is a living remembrance of Jesus and his revelation of God. The meaning of liturgy is expressed well in the ancient Latin hymn written by St. Thomas Aquinas, *O Sacrum Convivium*,

> *O sacrum convivium in quo Christus sumitur recolitur memoriae*
> *passonis ejus*
> O sacred banquet in which Christ is received and the
> memory of his passion is recalled
> *Mens impletur gratia nobis datur pignus futurae gloria*
> The mind is filled with grace and a pledge of future glory
> is given to us.

The past is recalled, the present is filled with grace, and all look forward to future glory. God has been good to people in the past; God is good to people in the present; God will be good to people in the future.

Preaching at liturgy must involve all three as well: the remembrance of God's relationship with people in the past, especially the giving of Jesus to the world; the present need for God's presence in human life; and the promise for the future.

THE CONTEXT: THE CONGREGATION

Preaching involves a particular congregation at a particular time. Generic preaching never works. A suburban congregation differs considerably from a city congregation. Preaching to children or adolescents differs from preaching to adults. Wealthy congregations form a different audience than poorer congregations. Well-educated people need a different explanation of the scriptures than less educated audiences. A congregation in a nursing home demands a different approach than one on a college campus. The good preacher tailors the preaching to the particular audience.

The occasion also affects the preaching. Funerals, weddings, baptisms, Christmas, Easter, or the summer celebrations of Memorial Day, the Fourth of July, and Labor Day all form a particular context within which people live and so within this same context the preaching will live. Talking about abortion on Mother's Day accomplishes nothing. Preaching about the solemnity of Mary on January 1 when the context of the congregation is New Year's Day probably accomplishes little. Preaching on faith and hope following a natural disaster makes more sense than preaching about the seven capital sins. Specific times, places, and congregations all must fit together in the mind of the preacher and in the actual preaching of the Word of God.

REVELATION: THE FOUNDATION FOR PREACHING

Revelation means an unveiling. What was unknown becomes known. In a more specific understanding the unveiling, the revelation, involves an offer of a relationship. When someone unveils himself or herself to another, the disclosure of some aspect of the person is an implicit offer of a relationship. The teacher reveals himself or herself, offering to students the relationship of student to teacher. When someone meets another for the first time the unveiling, the disclosure, is an offer of possible friendship. Sometimes the offer is accepted and other times rejected. If the initial offer is accepted, further unveiling takes place on the part of both individuals.

On the divine level, God offers a relationship to people. God unveils or discloses something of the meaning of being God and people either accept or reject. The acceptance is faith. Certainly God offers this relationship in diverse ways. Creation itself can be an implicit offering of a relationship to the Creator. When individuals have religious experi-

29

ences in life, this too is an offer of a relationship. Most times, or initially for many people, the offer of a relationship on the part of God is deeply personal and internal. But the relationship can also be made public and external. When one comes to faith through another or through an appreciation of another's religious experience, then the offer of the relationship to God fulfills the criteria to be public and external.

In the history of Israel, God offered a relationship to Abraham, Isaac, and Jacob, and especially through Moses, to the Jewish people. Moses had his religious experience in the desert, as did the Jewish people. The Old Testament records this offer of a relationship by God in which the people of Israel accept God's offer and become the people of God. The prophets also had their experience of God and they, in turn, reminded the people of Israel of their relationship to God and their need to live according to the faithful acceptance of this relationship.

In the New Testament, Jesus also has his experience of God in which he calls God "Abba," "Father." Like the Old Testament, the New Testament records the relationship between Jesus and God and also the relationship between God and the followers of Jesus through Jesus himself. People today turn to the New Testament to try to understand this record of the offer and the acceptance in faith. Once this is understood even partially, then the individual today can relate to his or her own need to accept a relationship to God.

The preacher knows the Bible, the record of the offer, and the response of the relationship by God to Israel, Jesus, and Christians. The preacher also has some awareness of the needs of the congregation and brings the two together. People today are aware of their need for God and of the offer of a relationship, but also need assistance in responding to this offer. The preacher offers that assistance.

Homiletics presupposes an eternal and ever-present offer by God of a relationship to people. Revelation forms the foundation for any preaching and demands an effort to know the history of the offer of a relationship to Israel, Jesus, and Christians. When people today understand something of the religious experience of those who have preceded them in faith, they can better deal with their own response to God's offer. Without revelation, the offer of the relationship is impossible. Without the record of this offer and response in the Bible and without an awareness of the needs of a contemporary congregation, preaching fails completely.

Homiletics has become more complicated and more demanding than initially thought. The personality, talents, and weaknesses of the preacher are involved. The content presupposes a good knowledge of the Bible. The context of liturgy colors the preaching, as does the congregation. Finally, all preaching involves the offer by God and the response of an individual and a community to this offer of a relationship to God. Each element forms only a part of the full meaning of preaching, but together they create the possibility of God being ever more present in the lives of people. The task is awesome, challenging, and satisfying. It is possible through the power of God, who continues to offer the possibility of a relationship through the preacher or even, at times, in spite of the preacher. God's Word goes forth and accomplishes its task. The preacher only serves that powerful Word.

B. The Homily

People need an encounter with the Word of God. This encounter need not of necessity be through the Bible since revelation involves more than its record in sacred scripture. For most people, however, whether of the Jewish or Christian religious tradition, the ordinary way in which people experience the Word of God is through the Bible. God offers salvation, that overwhelming experience of God's presence in human life, to all, *now*. Salvation is not reserved for an afterlife but is part of people's everyday experience. The awareness of God's Word, especially through Jesus, helps people to accept as fact the actual saving presence of God in human life. The Bible gives the assurance that this promised salvation is actually experienced. The homily serves this purpose.

WHAT THE HOMILY IS NOT

People, both preachers and listeners, often are confused by the word *homily* and thus fail to understand its meaning. A true homily is not a presentation of personal views. It does not provide an opportunity for the preacher to vent personal thoughts, opinions, or feelings, but it does involve the preacher and thus is personal.

The homily is not a theological lecture. People study theology in their own time and space or study theology through formal classes. Theology is faith seeking understanding. The homily does not provide the professor of theology an opportunity to expound on important or minor theological opinions, but it must presuppose good theology. To the lecture hall belongs theology. To the pulpit belongs the fruit of theology.

Just as the homily is not a theological lecture, neither is it detailed exegesis of a text. The careful study of the Bible involves the meaning of words, the literary genre used in the passage, an awareness of the theology of each book, as well as the interrelatedness of the books within the Bible. Good exegesis takes time and can often become quite tedious. The homily does not afford an occasion for complete biblical exegesis but instead presumes the exegetical foundation.

Sometimes preachers get involved in political and social issues. The homily does not mean a discussion of such views, however necessary for public life. Specific political or social issues belong to the domain in the church, but the Sunday homily is not the occasion to expound church teaching on social justice or political commitment. Yet, the homily has to be related to a real world, which contains political and social aspects.

Finally, the homily is not instructions on morality. Religious education, especially that which takes place in the home, offers the moral guidance necessary for life. When people come to church, a commitment to morality has already been integrated into each individual's life. The homily, however, does encourage moral activity and should always conclude with some resolution.

WHAT IS A HOMILY?

A homily is sacramental and symbolic activity uniting the Liturgy of the Word with the Liturgy of the Eucharist in the context of daily life. As sacramental activity, the homily involves God's action through the Word. As symbolic activity, the homily includes speaking, listening, and responding. Both preacher and listener are brought into contact with the saving presence of God through the Word of God as recorded in scripture related to the ordinary aspect of human daily life.

Listening to the Word of God precedes and finds its completion in the celebration of the presence of Jesus as God's Word in the reception of the Eucharist. One presupposes the other, and each relates to the other. The Word of God as proclaimed and then received in a sacred meal brings about a unity not only between God and people of faith through Jesus, but also accomplishes a unity among the people of faith themselves. Word and sacrament are not disparate entities but complementary or two facets of the same reality. Every homily should be related to the reception of the sacramental activity, especially the celebration of the Eucharist.

Finally, the homily must contribute to the daily lives of people. Most people live ordinary lives and are not the "movers and shakers" of the world. Most lives are commonplace. Surely the Word of God should figure into global decisions involving international justice or world hunger or peace, but most people have little to do with such overwhelming responsibilities. People live ordinary lives with thoughts, hopes, feelings, emotions, and an awareness of the need for others and an ever-developing sense of oneself. The homily must assist these people to enrich their lives by the acceptance of the Word of God.

So what does a preacher do? Know the Bible. Know the congregation. Offer some help to ordinary people living ordinary lives in accepting and living out their relationship to God. Present the meaning of a particular reading; place it in the context of the book from which it was taken; relate this meaning to the context of the congregation; and offer some suggestions for a response. To accomplish this the preacher:

1. Finds time each week to study the Bible. Reads the upcoming Sunday readings on Monday; thinks about them; uses sources for interpretations.

2. Spends time with the congregation, both good times as well as sad times.

3. Reads the newspapers, watches television, and so on. Knows what is going through the minds of the members of the congregation.

4. Develops an outline for the homily: the reading, the context of the reading, the context of the congregation, the desired response.

5. Relates the spoken word of God to the presence of the Word of God in the Eucharist.

6. Knows a preacher's strengths and weaknesses. Capitalizes on the strengths and tries to overcome the weaknesses.

7. Above all, sets some time apart each week to study the Bible.

B. The Homily

The good homilist knows the particular text, places it in the context from which it came, paying attention to its theology as part of the larger book of the Bible. The homilist also pays careful attention to the context of the congregation: what they are thinking and experiencing at that moment of time, and seeks a fitting response to suggest to the congregation—text, context, context of the congregation, and response.

Above all, the homilist sees the homily as contributing to the offer of a relationship by God to people. The preacher offers the one Word of God: God is present and God loves. If God has given Jesus present now in Word and sacrament, is there anything God will not give us? (Rom 8:32).

III.

THE GOSPEL OF JOHN

A. The Theology and the Community of the Gospel of John

Preaching any book of the Bible presupposes an understanding of the particular book: its purpose, how its understanding came from and influenced the original community, and how it might affect a believing community today. The Gospel of John bears witness not just as the work of an individual, but an individual who founded, guided, taught, and lived within a community of believers at the end of the first Christian century. Today, most refer to this individual as the Beloved Disciple. Although probably not one of the twelve apostles, he knew Jesus as an eyewitness and gathered followers of Jesus, and from this community the Gospel of John continues to bear witness to the Jesus tradition.

A SECULAR APPROACH TO CHRISTIANITY

Secular implies an emphasis on this present world and the "now moment." The Gospel of John conveys just such an approach to life and to faith. Rather than the love of God and neighbor, this gospel emphasizes human relationships alone: the love of the brethren, members of the community. The evangelist also teaches eternal life, now and not reserved for the future. "This is eternal life to know the one true God and him whom he has sent" (John 17:3).

The gospel shows an unusual Christian community. The members do not love the world: "Do not love the world or the things in the world. If anyone loves the world, the love of the father is not in him" (1 John 2:15). Jesus does not pray for the world (John 17:9), but rather that his followers may live in the world and not be part of it (John 17:14–16). Only those who recognize the voice of the Good Shepherd can follow him (John 10:3). Other sheep belong to the shepherd, but they must learn to hear the voice of the Lord and join those who already belong (John 10:16). The sense of belonging to the community binds each individual to the Lord as it binds them to each other in love. If individuals choose to leave the community, clearly they never belonged: "They went out from us but they were not of us; for if they had been of us, they would have continued with us; but they went out that it might be plain they are not of us" (1 John 2:19).

Even the commandment of love—"Love one another as I have loved you" (John 13:34)—seems limited and sectarian. The followers of the Lord are not commanded to love their enemies. First, they must love the brethren, those who belong to the community. The author has evidently experienced a close-knit group of believers who emphasized the need for a commitment to the Lord in faith and a profound love of the brethren that binds people together as one flock under one shepherd.

The Johannine community shared the same general beliefs of other Christian communities at the end of the century, but separated themselves from other followers of the Lord through their own interpretation of the Jesus tradition. As a community, they chose to emphasize the essentials: faith and love. Only then would they permit other Christian practices to exist.

COMMUNITY WITH DIVERSITY

Middle Eastern society at the end of the first century offered something for everyone. Judaism existed with various divisions especially after the destruction of the Temple in AD 70. Mystery religions with strange rituals attracted many with their promise of salvation. Early Gnosticism, the heresy that promised salvation through the communication of secret knowledge, had many adherents both within Judaism and Christianity. Greek philosophy offered everything from the delight of Epicureanism to the rigidity of Stoicism. Commerce flourished with the ever present Roman might. Even nascent Christianity had its divisions. Since no person can flee from societal influences but must pick and choose those that are helpful and avoid those that are

their
turn

harmful, the Johannine community had to learn to live in a diverse society and carve out its own sphere of influence. The community was composed of individuals. Thus, many of the above influences would be present in the community. Some people joined the community and later left, which further contributed to the sectarian nature of the group.

GROUPS OF PEOPLE IN THE COMMUNITY [milieu]

The gospel text gives evidence of several groups of people that formed part of the milieu of the Johannine community. Raymond Brown discovers five such groupings. The first was the opposition. Some individuals belonged to the "world" just as the members of the community did not belong to the "world." The title encompasses more than just the Jews who refused to believe in Jesus. For the Johannine community, these people deliberately chose to remain in the darkness. They lived under the influence of Satan, the prince of darkness and the prince of this world. Their presence in the milieu would have further contributed to the feeling on the part of the Johannine community of being strangers in the midst of those who chose darkness.

A second group, associated with the former, but distinct because of tradition and opportunity, was the Jews. They never accepted Jesus and persecuted any Jew who professed belief in him. From this group we have the decision, sometime around AD 85, to exclude from the synagogue anyone who acknowledged Jesus as the Messiah. The Johannine Christian teaching that Jesus was one with the Father, as well as their teaching that he had replaced the Temple, and thus its sacrifices, pointed a blow toward the heart of Judaism that had to be resisted.

At this period, we also have those who believed that John the Baptist, not Jesus, was the Messiah. The Johannine Christians reduce the importance of John; he becomes a witness to Jesus who acknowledges that he must decrease while Jesus increases.

Others were "crypto-Christians." They chose to remain in the synagogue but privately believed in Jesus. They tried to live in both camps, preferring the praise of men to the glory of God. Eventually, especially with the decision of the Jews to include in their prayers accusations against the followers of Jesus, these crypto-Christians would have to

A

B.

C.

D.

make a decision to publicly profess faith in Jesus or return to a full participation in the faith of the synagogue.

The divergent views on Christology uncover yet another group. These Jewish Christians accepted Jesus as a miracle worker sent by God, but did not acknowledge the high Christology advocated by the author of the gospel. For the evangelist, these individuals could not be seen as true believers even if they could trace their acceptance of Jesus to the community in Jerusalem. Initially, it would be acceptable to view Jesus as a miracle worker, but such a faith of necessity had to develop into the acceptance of Jesus as the eternal Son of God.

The final group of Christians that appears within the Johannine tradition are those of other apostolic churches. These believers traced their origin to Peter and the Twelve. They had developed a moderately high Christology emphasizing the origin of Jesus as the miraculous intervention of God in human history, but without explaining his precise relationship to God. Their ecclesiology also was a slight variance from the Johannine approach. Too often, for the Johannine community, they were occupied with corollaries to Christianity instead of emphasizing the essentials of faith and love. They had organization and an authority structure but did not pay sufficient attention to the faith commitment to Jesus and the love of the members of the community.

PROBLEMS IN THE COMMUNITY

The existence of these distinct groups helps to appreciate some of the problems faced by the Johannine community. In John 9:22, the reference to expulsion from the synagogue comes not from the time of the ministry of Jesus but from the period of the Johannine community. Eventually, Christians had to make a break with the synagogue. This decisive step on the part of Judaism forced the crypto-Christians to make a decision for or against the new way of Jesus.

The presence of followers of John the Baptist still claiming that he was the Messiah and not Jesus, prompted the Johannine community to downplay the importance of John and depict him not as the Baptizer (the term is not used) but as a Christian witness who bears testimony to Jesus.

A. The Theology and the Community of the Gospel of John

Even today some Christians tend to make the body of Jesus unreal. In the minds of some, he was God's Son who masqueraded as a man in a type of charade. Docetism, an early Christian heresy, held that the body of Jesus was not really a human body. The Johannine Gospel attempted to counteract this problem by emphasizing the reality of the body of Jesus in his ministry. Jesus thirsts, is hungry, and becomes tired. Even after the resurrection, he eats with his disciples.

Gnosticism, that strange system of beliefs, created an intellectual elite promising salvation through the communication of secret knowledge. The Gospel of John has some Gnostic influence: "The truth will make you free" (John 8:32) seems Gnostic. Jesus teaches what he has learned from his Father for he is the light of the world. This seems esoteric. Moreover he says that: "I am the way, the truth, and the light" (John 14:6). While some Gnostic influence may exist in this gospel, ultimately the evangelist teaches that the human race experiences salvation not through knowledge but through love.

Since the community lived in such a diverse environment, some of these influences find their way into the gospel, but also the basic thrust of the author's understanding of salvation remains constant. Jesus is glorified in his dying; salvation through the communication of the Spirit comes only through the death on the cross. "When I am lifted up, I will draw all men to myself" (John 12:32).

The community also faced problems with other Christian communities. By the end of the first century, the Christian church had sufficiently developed to institutionalize certain ecclesial offices. The more charismatic type of church order gave way to an established authority and hierarchy. Certain church leaders traced their office in the church to Peter and laid claim to a share in the authority of Jesus himself. The Johannine community came into conflict with these interpretations of Christianity and attempted to offer its own formula for church order. The third letter of John, verses 9–11, implies that other Christian communities had difficulties with the Johannine community. The interpretation of Christian faith by the community of the Beloved Disciple differed from other early communities and thus, inevitably, disagreements and dissensions created a troubled existence.

JOHANNINE DUALISM

The dualistic language of the Fourth Gospel invites further analysis as to its meaning and origin: light and darkness, truth and falsehood, above and below, good and evil, life and death, God and the world. Do these concepts come from a Gnostic background or are they rooted in Judaism? Some scholars have presented arguments in favor of the Gnostic origin for this dualism, while others have argued for the essential Jewish origin especially through the influence of the Qumran. The same concepts existed in Gnosticism as well as the Qumran and since the Johannine community flourished in a mixed social order, no one answer can be found to this question of origin. The Gnostic concept of life may very well have influenced the gospel. The general agreement in terminology in both the Qumran scrolls and the Fourth Gospel also shows a familiarity by the Johannine community of the thought present in the writings of the Qumran community even if no evidence for a direct literary dependence can be found.

The eclectic and sectarian form of heterodox Judaism of the Qumran best represents the intellectual environment from which the author of the Fourth Gospel discovered some of the language and concepts that he used to articulate his unusual formulation of the Christian message.

When contemporary students of John read of the struggle between light and darkness, good and evil, the world below and the world above, they must see these ideas coming from a group of people who are removed from the mainstream of social life; they expect to discover salvation through a personal relationship with God's envoy. The Qumran community withdrew from the orthodox way of Jewish life to a desert community in which they were dependent upon a teacher and waited expectantly for the coming of the Messiah who would usher in the final relationship to God. The Johannine community also withdrew from the mainstream developing Christianity and accepted a Christian faith that allowed for no compromise. They too awaited a fulfillment, but one that had substantially begun through the coming of Jesus.

JOHN AND THE SYNOPTICS

Any appreciation of the milieu of the Fourth Gospel must also include some investigation of the relationship between this gospel and the other three. Mark, Matthew, and Luke were in existence at this period of history and were accepted as authentic expressions of the Jesus tradition. Did the Johannine community use these gospels in any way?

Often in the past people looked upon the Fourth Gospel as an effort by John to fill in what was missing in the Synoptics. Today, such a theory has been dismissed. A careful study of the gospel shows no literary dependence by John on the other three. The Fourth Gospel seems closer to Luke and Mark than to Matthew, but even when examining the common elements between John, Luke, and Mark no evidence can be found for a direct literary dependence. The author of John most likely did not know the other three gospels, and the similarities can be explained by a comparable oral tradition that lies behind all of the gospels. The plan of the last gospel conforms to that of Mark—Galilee, Jerusalem, death and resurrection, the sending of the Spirit—but how the author presents this basic plan differs significantly.

ORDER OF EVENTS

The order of events changes in this gospel. The cleansing of the Temple, for example, takes place at the beginning of the ministry of Jesus rather than at the end, just before his death. John can situate this event here because, unlike the Synoptics, John has Jesus visiting Jerusalem several times and, thus, can locate the cleansing at one of the visits.

John also places the crucifixion on a different day. The Fourth Gospel sets the crucifixion on the day of preparation for the Passover, at the time the lambs would have been slain in the Temple in preparation for the Passover meal. For the Synoptics, Jesus celebrated the Passover meal with his disciples and then died the following day.

The author also presents the words of Jesus in a manner different from the Synoptics. All of the evangelists adapted the actual words of Jesus to suit the needs of the individual communities, but the authors of the Synoptic Gospels had a more conservative approach in preserving the historical words of Jesus. In the Fourth Gospel, half of the verses are discourses unknown to the Synoptics. John also seems to arrange and alter the words of Jesus with greater freedom. He presented the teaching of Jesus, but the words are those of the evangelist or perhaps of the Beloved Disciple.

The Beloved Disciple or the evangelist did not just create these discourses of Jesus. The so-called Johannine thunderbolt shows a common understanding among the evangelists: "All things have been delivered to me by my Father and no one knows the Son except the Father, and no one knows the Father except the Son and anyone to whom the Son chooses to reveal him" (Matt 11:27). The terminology is closer to that used in the Gospel of John, which would encourage any reader to recognize that the basic ideas in the Gospel of John are also present in the Synoptic tradition even if in a germinal or indirect fashion. In the Fourth Gospel, a reader discovers a creative remembering of the Jesus tradition that adapts the teaching of Jesus to the needs of a particular church community.

THE RISEN LORD SPEAKS

Throughout this gospel, as distinct from the other evangelists, the author presents Jesus as speaking from eternity. The Risen Lord addresses his followers more so than does the historical Jesus. The teaching is rooted in the earthly Jesus but carries a greater development. When the author, for example, narrates the miracle of the loaves in chapter 6, he presents the event in the context of Jesus as incarnate wisdom as well as Jesus present in the Eucharist. This differs significantly from Mark's presentation of the same miracle in chapters 6 and 8 in which Mark presents Jesus as the shepherd who feeds his flock and offers the food of the eschatological banquet.

All of the miracles of Jesus take on a different nuance in this gospel. In the Synoptics, they cause wonder. In the Fourth Gospel, they become signs, deeds of the earthly Jesus that involve faith in him not as just another miracle worker, but carry as well a pledge of the future outpouring of the Spirit.

The Jesus in this gospel differs significantly from the Jesus of the Synoptics. He is never without his glory, and this glory his followers have seen: "And we have seen his glory, glory as of the only Son from the Father" (John 1:14). In the earlier gospels, the authors offered no hint of preexistence. In Philippians 2:6, Paul hints at preexistence, but for John the Word was with God from the beginning and even when the Word became flesh, the Word remained in the bosom of the Father (John 1:18).

Since Jesus speaks from eternity, he knows everything. He knew Nathaniel under the fig tree (John 1:48); knew the Samaritan woman's marital status (John 4:17–18); knew his betrayer (John 6:70–71); knew when his hour had come to depart from this world (John13:1); was aware of all that would befall him as he was apprehended in the garden (John 18:4); and, finally, knowing that he had accomplished all, uttered, "I thirst," to fulfill the scriptures, and handed over his Spirit (John 19:28). No wonder he caused misunderstanding for Nicodemus, the Samaritan woman, and his disciples.

Jesus also knew no pain. No agony in the garden takes place. Jesus carries his own cross and moves to Calvary as in a glorious parade. Jesus reigns from the cross in perfect control of all that happens. The author did not set out to correct or amplify the Synoptics but, accepting teachings from the common oral tradition, developed his own approach to the Jesus tradition that was suited to the needs of his particular Christian community.

CONCLUSION

This survey of the milieu of the Fourth Gospel should make it evident to the reader that we have a syncretistic background. The community was sectarian; it flourished within a Christian environment that experienced internal as well as external problems; it had its opponents and critics; borrowed ideas and terminology from the heterodox Judaism of the Qumran community as well as Old Testament theology; relied on an oral tradition that was similar to the Synoptics, especially Luke and Mark, but in the end produced a document far different from any other gospel. The community's experience included current religious motifs but also had, of necessity, to deal with philosophical, political, sociological, and psychological elements. Freedom, individuality, clustering around a charismatic teacher called the Beloved Disciple, the experience of separateness, all are involved with psychology as well as sociology, and each element will find some expression in this gospel.

The work of recent scholarship has focused on these influences, and, thus, the preacher can better understand the gospel if he keeps the milieu in mind. As the preacher reads the gospel, he will be able to detect the currents described herein and begin to appreciate the genius and the value of this authentic witness to the meaning of Jesus.

B. Faith and Love: Foundations of the Community

The original ending of the Fourth Gospel expressly states its purpose:

> Jesus performed many other signs as well, signs not recorded here, in the presence of his disciples. But these have been recorded to help you believe that Jesus is the Messiah, the Son of God, so that through this faith you may have life in his name. (John 20:30–31)

On these verses alone, because of some textual problems in the verb, no one can determine whether the gospel reflects a missionary purpose, an attempt to enkindle faith in those who do not yet believe, or a homiletic purpose: to strengthen and confirm that faith of an already constituted congregation. These verses, however, emphasize the importance of faith to the author and inspirer of the gospel. They also will encourage the preacher to use this gospel to strengthen and support the faith in the Christian community, as well as to enkindle faith in those who might be interested in Christianity.

Faith in the Fourth Gospel is the human response to the revelation of Jesus. This faith consists of an active acceptance, seen in the author's choice of a verb "to believe" rather than just the noun, "belief." Jesus demands a decision as he encounters individuals. The individual becomes aware of need and the reality of sin and darkness. When Jesus enters into the individual's life, the person loses all false illusions and accepts the salvation offered. The believer accepts Jesus not just as a miracle worker but as the Son of God. Once accepted personally, the words of Jesus become revelatory and lead to acceptance by the Father.

God the Father also plays a significant role in the birth of faith. The Father gives the disciples to Jesus and then draws the disciples to faith

49

in Jesus and actually teaches them through the words of Jesus. Faith in this gospel becomes a gift of God the Father:

> All that the Father gives to me will come to me; and he who comes to me I will not cast out. (John 6:37)

The author knows of the close relationship between Jesus and God. The Father has sent him into the world. He knows also the need for a divine initiative if an individual can recognize the presence of God the Father through Jesus and his preaching:

> Philip said to him, "Lord, show us the Father and we shall be satisfied." Jesus said to him, "Have I been with you so long and yet you do not know me, Philip? He who has seen me has seen the Father." (John 14:8–9)

> He who believes in me, believes not in me but in him who sent me. And he who sees me sees him who sent me. (John 12:44–45)

God the Father speaks to the heart of the person, which enables the individual to accept Jesus as the personal revelation of God.

BELIEVING AND KNOWING

The relationship between Jesus and the Father in the origin and content of faith becomes especially evident in a study of the words *believing* and *knowing*. Nearly two hundred times the author uses the words *to believe* or *to know*. Often he uses figurative references that at times say more, and other times say less, than the literal words. Coming to the light is a figurative expression of faith in Jesus; hearing the voice of the Good Shepherd and recognizing it, is a figurative expression within a parable. Remaining close to the vine in the parable of the vine and the branches also expresses the relationship of faith. Believing and knowing, and coming to Jesus and staying with him, are personal activities that pervade the entire gospel. The major and minor personages in the gospel manifest how some believe and others do not; some know him and others fail to recognize him. His disciples appear under every possible heading: fluctuating, changing, and making faltering advances, as they come to believe and to know Jesus as God's personal envoy and their personal Lord and Savior.

The opening chapter of the gospel already presents the image of light coming into a dark world calling people to faith: "In him was life and the life was the light of men. The light shines in the darkness and the darkness has not overcome it" (John 1:4–5).

> But to all who received him, who believed in his name, he
> gave power to become children of God. (John 1:12)

This same chapter narrates the call of the first disciples. In each instance, immediately, they make a profession of faith. Andrew tells his brother Peter: "We have found the Messiah" (John 1:41). Philip tells Nathaniel: "We have found him of whom Moses in the law and also the prophets wrote" (John 1:45). Nathaniel declares: "Rabbi, you are the Son of God, you are the king of Israel" (John 1:49). This opening chapter also situates the role of John the Baptist. He simply bears testimony to Jesus as the Lamb of God and encourages his own disciples to follow Jesus (John 1:29–34).

Nicodemus comes from the darkness troubled by Jesus. He knows Jesus represents more than just a miracle worker: "No one can do these signs that you do unless God is with him" (John 3:2). But Nicodemus does not make his profession of faith. He appears again in John 7:50, at the meeting of the Sanhedrin, and displays a concern for Jesus that he be treated according to the law. Finally, in John 19:39 he helps prepare the body of Jesus for burial. His interest and concern for Jesus could be contrasted with the Samaritan woman who is receptive to Jesus and, ultimately, not only makes her profession of faith, but also becomes an evangelist, inviting her townspeople to listen to Jesus:

> They said to the woman, "It is no longer because of your
> words that we believe, for we have heard for ourselves
> and we know that this is indeed the Savior of the world."
> (John 4:42)

Judas, of course, receives every opportunity to believe, to come to the light, but he preferred the darkness. At the Last Supper, he left the upper room and the evangelist tells us: "And it was night" (John 13:30). Jesus will not force anyone to believe in him. Faith is God's gift, which must be accepted in personal freedom.

The Jews, the leaders of the people, also had their opportunity to believe. Jesus taught daily in the temple. When questioned by the high priest Jesus responded:

> I have spoken openly to the world; I have always taught in synagogues and in the temple, where all Jews come together. I have said nothing secretly. (John 18:20)

But for this group, faith in Jesus became impossible. They could not recognize the presence of the God of Abraham, Isaac, and Jacob in Jesus and ultimately denied their heritage at the trial of Jesus. When Pilate asked the Jews: "Shall I crucify your King?" (John 19:15), the leaders answered: "We have no king but Caesar" (John 19:15). In the history of Israel, God alone was their true king and even when they had an earthly king, his presence represented their true king, God. The Jews in the passion of the Lord not only fail to come to faith in Jesus, but actually reject their own faith as expressed in the Old Testament.

THE FAITHFUL DISCIPLES

The disciples of the Lord, as they appear in his ministry, also exemplify the various conditions of faith. Peter, the Mother of the Lord, Thomas, the Beloved Disciple, Martha and Mary, and Mary Magdalene—they become symbolic figures, representing not just their own level of belief, but also offering to other Christian communities an example and help in understanding the origin, value, and meaning of faith.

THE CONTENT OF FAITH

In every chapter the objects of faith and knowledge are Jesus and his mission. The object of knowing, however, is different in this gospel from the object of believing. When the author uses the words *to know*, he rarely uses simple nouns or pronouns. These are common, however, with the use of the words *to believe*. "To believe in," with an accusative, has God as the object in two instances: "He who believes in me believes not in me but in him who sent me" (John 12:44); "Let not your hearts be troubled; believe in God, believe also in me" (John 14:1). In all other instances, individuals are asked to believe in Jesus.

When the author uses the verb *to believe* with a dative, the objects are transitional; they are testimonies, words of Jesus or signs. In each case, the signs point to the meaning of the mission of Jesus: "They believed the scripture and the word Jesus had spoken" (John 2:22); "Even though you do not believe me, believe the works that you may know and understand that the Father is in me and I am in the Father" (John 10:38).

The results of believing and knowing Jesus are eternal life or the entering into eternal life: "And this is eternal life that they know thee the only true God and Jesus Christ whom thou has sent" (John 17:3); "Whoever believes in him should not perish but have eternal life" (John 3:16). The individual believes in Jesus and his mission, comes to know him and who he is, and understands the mission of Jesus. Then the individual believes and possesses eternal life.

The author of John stressed the relationship between believer and Jesus; he writes about the growth of faith, the role of the Father in bringing people to faith, and he speaks of the content of that faith: Jesus and his mission. The established purpose of the gospel, as given in John 20:31, helps individuals "to believe that Jesus is the Christ, the Son of God and that believing you may have life in his name." If no faith exists, then for the community of the Beloved Disciple, no Christian community exists. The essential need for this faith relationship is particularly expressed in the parable of the good shepherd.

THE GOOD SHEPHERD

The image of the shepherd and the flock appears frequently in Near Eastern literature. In the Old Testament, the Book of Numbers used the image of shepherd when Moses asked God for someone to share in his authority (Num 27:17). Zechariah used a similar image (Zech 11:4), and the prophet Ezekiel used the image of the shepherd not only for the leaders of Israel but also for God himself (Ezek 34).

Each of the Synoptics used the same image. Mark presented Jesus as the shepherd: "I will strike the shepherd and the sheep will be scattered" (Mark 14:27). Matthew recorded the parable of the lost sheep (Matt 18:12–14). Finally, Luke used the image in two places: Jesus referred to his disciples as a flock: "Fear not little flock, for it is your Father's good pleasure to give you the kingdom" (Luke 12:32), and chapter 15 records the parable of the lost sheep (Luke 15:3–7).

What characterizes the parable of the good shepherd in the Gospel of John is the reciprocal relationship between Jesus and the individual sheep. The sheepfold is unified by Jesus alone. Jesus has a close and intimate relationship with each sheep, grounded on the union and relationship between Jesus and his Father. The chapter actually contains two parables, that of the shepherd and the sheep, and the door and the sheepfold. In each instance the author presents the parable and then explains its meaning:

> The sheep hear his voice as he calls his own by name and leads them out. When he has brought out all those that are his, he walks in front of them, and the sheep follow him because they recognize his voice. They will not follow a stranger; such a one they will flee, because they do not recognize a stranger's voice. (John 10:3b–5)

This parable finds its explanation after the author has interpreted the meaning of the door and the sheepfold:

> I am the good shepherd; the good shepherd lays down his life for the sheep. The hired hand, who is no shepherd nor owner of the sheep, catches sight of the wolf coming and runs away, leaving the sheep to be scattered by the wolf. That is because he works for pay; he has no concern for the sheep. I am the good shepherd. I know my sheep and my sheep know me in the same way that the Father knows me and I know the

Father; for these sheep I will give my life. I have other sheep that do not belong to this fold. I must lead them, too, and they shall hear my voice. There shall be one flock then, one shepherd. (John 10:11–16)

In the presentation of the first parable (John 3b–5), Jesus calls his sheep by name. They know his voice. He does not confuse them, and they feel secure with the sound of his voice. Calling by name has a long biblical tradition implying intimacy as well as power and influence. Jesus knows his sheep sufficiently well to call them personally by name. He unites the individual with himself, and the individual feels secure in following the Lord.

In the interpretation of the second parable (John 10:11–16), the intimate knowledge is again expressed. The Old Testament knew of the intimate knowledge that existed between God and the people of Israel: "He knows those who take refuge in him" (Nah 1:7). Jesus exemplifies this intimate knowledge, for through him, God expressed care for the flock. The mission of Jesus in this parable makes clear the intimacy that also exists between Jesus and his Father. Jesus is for God; he is nothing apart from what he is for God. Because of this, Jesus could claim to be the revealer of God. The full parable also brings out God being for Jesus. Because Jesus is united with his sheep, then God is also for the followers of the Lord.

UNITY

John 10:16 stresses the purpose of this knowledge: to bring all to unity. A mutual knowledge that exists between Jesus and God, and Jesus and the flock, unites the flock to God. For the author of John, this union of God and his envoy, Jesus, and the believer, makes eternal life possible for humanity. The sheep know the shepherd; the believer knows the Father and the one sent by the Father and, thus, the believer has eternal life: "And this is eternal life, that they know thee the only true God and Jesus Christ whom thou has sent" (John 17:3).

The unity that exists between Father and Son is also expressed by the phrase: the Son being in the Father and the Father being in the

Son (John 10:38; 14:11; 17:21); the author also uses the expression: "The Son knows the Father" (John 10:15; 17:25). Jesus as the Good Shepherd who knows his sheep implies a relationship that is similar to that of Jesus and the Father. As the Son knows the Father and receives life from him, so those who know the Son know the Father and receive eternal life. A stringent bond unites the individual believer with the Lord.

THE MEANING OF THE FLOCK

Commentators interpret the flock in many different ways. It appears that some of the sheep in the sheepfold are not of the flock of Jesus; only those who hear his voice belong to him. The image of many flocks in one sheepfold, each belonging to a different shepherd, fits the conditions of the time. In the morning, the different shepherds entered the fold, and the sheep that belonged to them followed them out to pasture. Such an interpretation of the parable could imply that the larger flock symbolized the Jews at the time of Jesus.

The reference to sheep that belong to other folds could further call to mind the Gentiles and their call to faith in Jesus. Still further, the flock may be interpreted as a community closely akin to the Gnostic myth of the revealer who gathers together the dispersed sparks of light present in every individual and unites these sparks into the original unity. As knowledge was the means by which the Gnostic redeemer united individuals and brought salvation, so it is the mutual knowledge of Jesus and his flock that brings salvation and eternal life.

Whatever the interpretation, the collectivity is evident even if some do not belong to the group. The flock is diversified with some united with Jesus (those who hear his voice). Others remain separated (those who do not respond to his voice). The flock also seems open to growth (other sheep outside). In the interpretation of the parable, Jesus is the sole principle of unity based upon his unity with the Father. The unity that exists among the sheep is only implicit. Since they have a personal relationship with the shepherd, they may also have a personal relationship among themselves, but this dimension remains in the background. The author chooses to stress, in this parable, the faith relationship between Jesus and the individual without discussing the relationship that also exists between believers.

The parable might mirror the historical situation of the call of Jesus to the Jews. It also may mirror the historical situation of the troubled Johannine community, separated from the synagogue, experiencing divisions within itself, as well as problems in relating to other Christian communities. The parable would recognize the divisions, but would also offer hope for a final unity in the future, both within the community and without.

This parable insists on the need to remain with Jesus as the leader and guide and to continue to respond to his voice. At first glance, the image of the shepherd and flock might appear to be an image of the church, but such a conclusion needs careful nuancing. The parable concerns a personal and individual relationship with Jesus. In that relationship, because of the image of a flock, some reference to a community exists but only implicitly. For John, no community exists unless first exist individual believers united with Jesus in faith.

The parable of the vine and the branches completes the author's call for the essentials, for in this parable the faith that unites the individual with Jesus finds its expression in the love that binds believers together.

THE LOVE OF THE BRETHREN

The Synoptic Gospels record the question put to Jesus by the inquiring scribe: "Which commandment is the first of all?" (Mark 12:28). Jesus responded with the well-known reply of the twofold commandment:

> The first is, "Hear O Israel: The Lord our God, the Lord is one; and you shall love the Lord your God with all your heart, and with all your soul, and with all your mind, and with all your strength." The second is this, "You shall love your neighbor as yourself." (Mark 12:29–31)

See also Matthew 22:34–40; Luke 20:39–40; 10:25–28.

Jesus quotes from Deuteronomy 6:4, the reference to the first commandment, and then from Leviticus 19:18, the reference to the love of neighbor. Each of the Synoptics recorded this incident in the life of the Lord, and from this teaching Christianity has developed its insistence on the close relationship between the love of God and the love of neighbor.

Matthew and Luke also enjoin the followers of the Lord to love their enemies: "Love your enemies and pray for those who persecute you" (Matt 5:44); "Love your enemies, do good to those who hate you, bless those who persecute you, pray for those who abuse you" (Luke 6:27–28). Luke continues his call to expand the commandment of love by expecting believers to turn the other cheek: give your cloak and your coat to the one who takes; give to all who beg; and do to others as you would wish others to do to you (Luke 6:29–31).

Christianity has flourished as a religion that offers love to all and will not discriminate even when the Christian faces rejection or persecution. The love of God and love of neighbor are irrevocably joined together. Matthew exemplifies this relationship when he records the words of Jesus:

> So if you are offering your gift at the altar and there remember that your brother has something against you, leave your gift there before the altar and go first to be reconciled to your brother. (Matt 5:23–24)

THE ONE COMMANDMENT IN JOHN

How strange that the author of John fails to record this twofold commandment! The Gospel of John emphasizes love but omits the two great commandments: "For the Father loves the Son" (John 5:20) and will love those who keep the commandments of the Lord and who respond to his Word. Together Jesus and his Father will come to those who love him (John 14:21–24). The author joins together the love of God for the Son and then completes the love relationship by including in that love all who come to believe in the Son. The mission of Jesus itself manifests the love of God for humankind: "For God so loved the world that he gave his only Son" (John 3:16). And the Father loves the Son precisely because the Son as the Good Shepherd will lay down his life to take it up again (John 10:15). All of these sayings, however, do not deal with the love that should exist among the disciples.

Instead of teaching two commandments, John tells his followers that Jesus demands only one:

> A new commandment I give to you that you love one another; even as I have loved you, you also love one another. By this all men will know that you are my disciples if you have love for one another. (John 13:34–35)

The author of First John directs his readers:

> If anyone says I love God and hates his brother, he is a liar; for he who does not love his brother whom he has seen, cannot love God whom he has not seen. (1 John 4:20)

The author of John knows that the love of God and neighbor belong together, but will emphasize that it is through the love of the brethren that followers can have the love of God. The one commandment of the Johannine community does not mean the love command itself, but the criteria by which the community will judge that love. No longer does the believer love the neighbor as oneself. The followers of Jesus must love the brethren as Jesus loved them. Since Jesus was the Good Shepherd who gave his life for the sheep, the followers of Jesus must love the brethren to the point of dying for a single member of the community.

The author also omits any reference to the love of enemy. The members of the Johannine community love the brethren, those who are members of the community. Unless the followers are joined together in a bond of love, flowing from the bond of faith that joins the individuals to Jesus, they will be unable to fulfill the further mission of Christianity to the world. The sectarian Johannine community banded together for mutual support and protection and, following the example of the Lord, they would willingly give up their lives for the sake of the brethren. If the parable of the good shepherd exemplified the faith relationship between Jesus and the individual believer, the parable of the vine and the branches completes this faith dimension by teaching the followers to bear fruit, to love one another.

THE VINE AND THE BRANCHES

Commentators often compare the two parables, the good shepherd with the vine and the branches. They have a similarity in structure and in theology. Both present a parable followed by an explanation, but the more significant comparison lies in the theology. Both parables manifest the close relationship between Jesus and the individual, but the first stresses the faith dimension. The parable of the vine and the branches emphasizes the conclusion of faith: the love of the brethren. This parable expands and explains the love of the brethren in chapter 13.

The chapter opens with a recognition formula, an identification of Jesus as the true vine, along with a reference to the activity of the Father. The Father calls disciples to faith. Here the Father prunes and cuts the branches to make them more fruitful. The meaning of fruitfulness, however, does not become clear until verse 12. In the opening verses of the parable, the chief participants are presented and interrelated: the Father who loves Jesus and who brings individuals to Jesus; the Son who loves the Father and his disciples; and finally the disciples themselves, as the branches that bear fruit by loving one another.

Unlike the parable of the good shepherd, chapter 15 presupposes faith: "You are already made clean by the word I have spoken to you" (John 15:3). The disciples already are related to the Lord by their faith commitment. The Lord now reminds them to remain close to him. With faith as the presupposition, the author can concentrate on the result of faith: the love of the brethren.

LOVE OF THE BRETHREN

The interpretation of the parable from verses 7 to 17 clarifies the need for love as the fulfillment of the command of Jesus, and makes evident the responsibility to give one's life for a member of the community. Faith becomes authentic only when it leads to love of Jesus (John

15:9–10) and the love one has for another (John 15:12–17). Only through the presence of love in the community can the mission of Jesus continue. The author juxtaposes both faith and love with mission, implying that the internal life of the community and its mission to the world are inseparable. If the believer wishes to fulfill the call to discipleship, this will be possible only through an internal love for the brethren that will include a willingness to give one's life:

> This is my commandment, that you love one another as I
> have loved you. Greater love has no man than this, that a
> man lay down his life for his friends. You are my friends if
> you do what I command you. (John 15:12–14)

The final verse of the interpretation of the parable culminates the discourse that sums up what Jesus has been saying. He returns to his simple command: "This I command you, to love one another" (John 15:17).

LIFE THROUGH JESUS

The parable stresses first the individual relationship to Jesus. While the word *life* is not mentioned, the notion is understood. Jesus is the source of life for the branches and so they must remain in him. No apparent relationship exists between branches. All receive their life from Jesus, the vine, and then each glorifies God by bearing fruit. The parable also contains the warning that a branch can be cut off and burned. Such an event has no effect on the other branches, which continue to remain united with Jesus. The individual must remain in Jesus.

The individual figures prominently in this parable, as well as in the good shepherd parable. The relationship of individuals within the community then becomes clearer. The command of Jesus to love one another binds the community together. The power of love moves from Father to Jesus, to the disciples, culminating in the mutual love of disciple for disciple. Faith finds its completion not only in the love of the Lord but also in the love of the brethren.

With these two parables, the Johannine community testifies to the essentials of Christianity: The community must have its foundation on a

2 key
concerns

personal commitment of faith to Jesus, and this faith must bear fruit. Without the personal acceptance of Jesus and the fulfillment of the command of love, there can be no Christian church.

JOHANNINE MYSTICISM

In chapter 15 the author interplays the "abiding with," or "being with," of the disciples and Jesus, and Jesus and God, and the disciples and God. Some call this *Johannine mysticism*. The same notion appears in the farewell discourses, especially in chapters 14 and 17. The author implies a mystical union between Jesus and the Father. Some sense of future union will involve all three participants:

> A little while now and the world will see me no more; but
> you will see me as one who has life, and you will have life.
> (John 14:19)

Because this author was aware of the importance of the present moment, this union was not divorced from history. The abiding of God through Jesus culminates and completes the fellowship made possible through faith. The future union was present in the earthly relationship between Jesus and his disciples. The fellowship had begun but would be perfected in a more intimate union when Jesus had been glorified:

> If a man loves me he will keep my word, and my Father will
> love him and we will come to him and make our home with
> him. (John 14:23)

Those who responded in faith entered into a special type of knowledge and love with Jesus and with the Father. The union joined not just the revealer and those to whom he revealed, but the very source of the revelation and the revelation itself: God the Father.

FAREWELL DISCOURSES

The need for a fruitful life of love on the part of the believers appears in other sections of the farewell discourses (chapters 13—17).

Mystical union and interiority appear in the first section of these discourses (John 13:31—15:10), while exterior expression and witness characterize the second section (John 15:12—16:33).

In the first section, the command of love figures prominently as seen previously in John 13:34. This follows the foot washing. It is not repeated again until John 15:12. The intervening verses stress mutual indwelling. Thirteen out of the fourteen times the author uses the words *to remain in* occur in this first section. The mutual indwelling of Father and Son, and Jesus and his disciples, occurs seven times.

Chapter 14 begins with the call to the disciples to believe in Jesus as they have believed in God and promises that the goal of the journey is the Father (John 14:12). Through Jesus, the disciples also will reach the Father and be with him (John 14:6, 23).

Chapter 15 continues the theme of mutual indwelling in spite of its abrupt ending. The development comes from a change in perspective. The author introduces the bearing of fruit as a result of the abiding in Jesus. The section climaxes in verse 10:

> You will live in my love if you keep my commandments, even as I have kept my Father's commandments, and live in his love. (John 15:10)

The focus of union and indwelling is the love of Jesus for his disciples, rooted in the love of the Father.

Johannine mysticism does not conclude in a sterile union but in an abiding presence that rests on responsible love directed outward to the brethren. The centrifugal force of love becomes centripetal. Finally, the author sees the love as the perfection and the completion of the union already present. Seeing and believing become knowing and loving and, ultimately, uniting and testifying.

THE ESSENTIALS OF CHRISTIANITY

The church results from belief in Jesus, which accomplishes a union of hearts and wills with the Father. The same love that binds Jesus to the Father, binds the Father to the followers, and the followers to each other. The one commandment of the Johannine Gospel is possible, because in its observance the individual experiences the love of God. Johannine mysticism, the relationship and union with God, demands a union of love among the brethren. Interiority becomes externalized in the community of believers.

THE WORLD

The need for a united community becomes more evident in contrast to the world. The section on hatred of the world (John 15:18—16:4) follows immediately after the mutual love explanation of the vine and the branches. The juxtaposition of these themes relates the stance of the disciples to the world, to that of Jesus himself. Jesus was rejected. The disciples will be rejected for the same reason: "They do not know the one who sent me" (John 16:3); the disciples will be expelled from the synagogue (John 16:2) and will be put to death (John 16:2b), "because they knew neither the Father nor me" (John 16:3b).

Jesus prepared his followers for rejection and persecution but only after he had made them secure in his love and the love of the Father. In the first section of the farewell discourses, Jesus asks his disciples to deepen their personal assimilation in faith to himself as the Son. The second half presents the disciples growing in their union with Jesus in his personal relationship to the Father and in his mission from the Father to the world. The love they bear for one another will be the sustaining power for them to continue this mission.

Previously, the author presented the orientation in faith as the work of the Father. The same idea occurs in the first section of the farewell discourses recalling the earlier statement: "No one can come to me unless the Father, who sent me, draws him" (John 6:44). In these final words before Jesus departs, the love that the disciples have for each other also has its origin in the love of God as Father. "For the Father himself loves you from the fact that you have loved me and have believed that I have come forth from the side of God" (John 16:28).

The disciples' knowledge of God, through love, leads them to recognize the nature of God. This also explains the presence of only one commandment in the Gospel of John, as well as the emphasis in 1 John on the need to love one another.

CONCLUSION FOR PREACHERS

The union of Jesus with his disciples through faith and love interacts with the command of love and the witness of the followers in the world. They make the Christian community different from any other type of religious community. For the author of this gospel, faith and love are essential. When they are present the Lord, his Spirit, and the Father are present. When these qualities are absent, there can be no Christian *Church* church. The role of faith, the command of love, and the mystical union that the author emphasizes in his gospel are all elements of the church. The evangelist does not present a complete ecclesiology in this gospel. Rather, he chose to present to his readers those elements that he saw as foundational for the church. For the Christian community of all ages, the Johannine community continues to bear testimony to the essentials of Christianity. Everything the church possesses, operates, or directs must have its foundation in the personal commitment to the Lord and the love of the brethren. Only then can the church fulfill its mission to all.

Preaching the Gospel of John rests on this understanding of the role of faith and the love of the brethren. The gospel stresses the individual. No real authority figure other than Jesus and the Spirit appear in this gospel. In the final chapter, Peter will share in the pastoral office of Jesus provided he loves Jesus and will die for the sheep.

The gospel is filled with symbolism, but alone among the gospels does not record the baptism of Jesus. Nor does the author narrate the institution of the Eucharist, although he has the longest section devoted to the Last Supper. For him sacraments express faith; otherwise they mean nothing.

Eternal life comes through faith and nothing more, and has begun when a person comes to faith and expects no further judgment other than coming to the light (John 5). The believer has passed from death to life.

C. The Jews in the Gospel of John

Over the centuries, many have noted the negative use of the word *Jews* in this gospel. For some, the Gospel of John, along with the Gospel of Matthew and his cry of "His blood be upon us and our children" (Matt 27:25), sets the foundation for anti-Semitism throughout the Christian era down to the present day. In an age when Christians, and Catholics, have become more sensitive to any accusation of anti-Semitism, particularly after the Second Vatican Council, many have tried to eradicate any sense of anti-Semitism from this gospel. Some claim that the gospel is anti-Jewish and not anti-Semitic, at least in the sense of Jewish authorities; while some have said that it refers not to "Jews," but to Judeans. Others see the use of "Jews" as ironic: the true "Jews" are the members of the Johannine community. Still others see the use of the word coming from the Jewish leaders, especially the Pharisees after the destruction of the Temple in the time of the Johannine community, rather than from the ministry of Jesus. Like many opinions regarding this gospel, perhaps the truth lies in all of the theories and in none of them completely.

The gospel does use the word *Jews* in a negative light. At least forty times the author uses it in a pejorative sense and only perhaps six or seven times uses it positively or, possibly, neutrally. At times, it might better be translated as Judeans, but clearly not in all cases. Irony is a characteristic of the gospel and may well be present here. And the Jewish authorities did oppose Jesus.

The Gospel of John, although at times considered the most Hellenistic of all of the gospels, more recently has been viewed by most scholars as the most Jewish. The influences come principally from Judaism, and in all likelihood the members of this community not only were predominantly Jewish Christians, but saw themselves as continuing to be Jewish even as they followed Jesus. Jesus was a Jew and the Messiah; his followers in this community maintained that commitment to Judaism.

To leave Judaism for a new religion took time. Not until well into the second century did Christianity become a predominant Gentile religion separated from Judaism. At that period, the Gospel of John would have been read in a different context, especially when it had also been adopted by the Gnostics as their own gospel. The gospel comes from within a Jewish rather than from within a Gentile Christian context. Originally, the anti-Jewish tone of the gospel probably was an intra-Jewish conflict. "My Judaism is better than your Judaism!"

Still, the "Jews" in this gospel more often represent the evil response of the "world" in rejecting both Jesus and his followers. It seems, however, that the author, a Jew himself, thought the Jews would have been more receptive to Jesus and his teachings, except for a strong and vocal elite among them who hindered belief in Jesus as the Messiah. Jesus himself is called a Jew, but only by non-Jews (Samaritan woman, John 4:9; Pilate, John 18:35). Jesus accepted the title even though his followers are not called "Jews."

By the time of the written gospel, followers of Jesus had been excluded from the synagogue, which caused a terrible rift in the lives of many of them. To be accused of not being a "Jew" would have had terrible psychological effects, including separation from family and friends. To counteract such an accusation, the Johannine community may well have accused the Jews, especially the religious leaders, of not being true Jews. For them, the true Jews were followers of Jesus, the Jewish Messiah.

Something similar exists today within Catholicism. Extreme right-wing Catholics call themselves true and orthodox Catholics, dismissing anyone who does not agree with them and who does not follow observances as well as they claim to do. Opponents consider themselves as the real Catholics and the orthodox Catholics as betraying the Catholic heritage of two thousand years.

John calls the religious authorities "Jews," ironically denying their right to set criteria for Jewish identity. The author frequently uses irony. Jesus was truly the king of the Jews, although not understood either by the religious authorities or by the Romans. Nicodemus, a

Jewish leader, does not come to faith and yet the Samaritan woman, rejected by the Jews, recognizes Jesus as the Messiah. Jesus is from heaven, yet from the Earth. Jesus does not pray for the world, and yet his disciples live in the world. The gospel teems with Johannine irony.

The "Jews" in this gospel are the Jewish religious leaders at the time of John's writing. After the destruction of the Temple, they strive to control Judaism: who belongs and who does not. They wish to exclude from Judaism any group they consider heterodox, which specifically meant the followers of Jesus. The authorities may call themselves Jews but they are not (Rev 2:9; 3:9). The author reads this conflict back into the time of Jesus and thus portrays the contemporary Jews of his time, continuing the opposition that Jesus felt in his own ministry. The Johannine Jewish Christians considered Christians to be the fulfillment of Judaism. They had trouble with the "Jews," the new religious leaders after the destruction of the Temple, because they saw themselves as the true "Jews," alone loyal to Jewish traditions as found in belief in Jesus as the Messiah.

Any writing must be understood in context. Reading the Gospel of John and noting the use of the word *Jews* should not be read in the context of two thousand years of anti-Semitism, but, rather, in the context of a conflict at the end of the first and beginning of the second centuries. Just who were the true Jews? The religious leaders at the time of John may call themselves Jews, but the true Jews are the followers of Jesus. If nothing more, preachers should be aware of the complex nature of the use of the term in the Fourth Gospel.

IV.

THE GOSPEL OF JOHN IN THE LECTIONARY

Third Sunday of Advent B

John 1:6–8, 19–28

John the Baptizer proclaims: "Prepare ye the way of the Lord," and becomes the great Advent saint. He appears on the scene briefly in the liturgical celebrations, announces his message, and disappears, not unlike his role in history. He announced the Lord; he leveled the hills and filled up the valleys to remove the obstacles that prevented people from hearing the Lord. Then he was forgotten; he decreased so that Jesus could increase.

The herald of the modern musical *Godspell* captures the mood of this Advent saint. The musical setting for "Prepare Ye the Way of the Lord" is plaintive and haunting. John came neither eating nor drinking, but called people to turn into themselves and see what is there. He wanted repentance, a change in thinking and living; he preached justice and integrity and clear principles; he wanted people to make room for the coming of the Lord. John had integrity. He examined himself in relationship to God and lived accordingly. He refused to compromise God's law and called for all of God's people to uphold that law. His integrity brought about his death. John could not remain silent when Herod married his brother's wife. Herod violated the law and so John died because he lived what he believed.

John lived lowly, unashamedly. He announced not himself but another and fulfilled his vocation. He did not try to establish an empire, a kingdom, a following. He knew his station in life and lived accordingly. When Jesus arrived on the scene, he willingly decreased. John courageously proclaimed a message of repentance. He never blanched in the presence of the powerful; he refused to water-down his message to make it more acceptable. He received clear directives from God to prepare for the coming of the Lord and boldly pinpointed some of the cancers of his society. John sought no personal gain but with confidence in the power of God lived out his life.

In the Fourth Gospel, John does not baptize Jesus. He is simply called "John" with no further designation. His only purpose is to point out Jesus. He fulfills his mission and then leaves the scene. In chapter 5 Jesus refers to John as a "bright and shining light" (John 5:35). The quality of his life and his dedication to his mission gave light to those who would follow his example.

PREACHER'S PREPARATION

The question of integrity and honesty could be stressed in the homily. Principles are too often compromised in life, and too many people pretend to be someone they are not. Every person has a mission to perform: living according to the gospel of Jesus in truth and honesty. John offers such an example.

John pointed out Jesus. Followers of Jesus today have the same ministry. They point out Jesus by living according to his teachings, especially following the example of John, by being truthful with themselves, and announcing another, not themselves.

Christmas Mass During the Day

John 1:1–18

Before the reform of the liturgy of the Second Vatican Council, Catholics heard this section of the gospel at the end of every Mass, and thus it was called the "last gospel." The poetry of this opening section of the Gospel of John has long mystified and charmed readers and listeners. The author crams all of the principal themes of the entire gospel into these verses.

The Word of God preexists; light and life and creation, wisdom, acceptance and rejection, the role of John the Baptist, and finally the Word of God becomes flesh and pitches his tent among us. All these references appear throughout the body of the gospel. With so many themes in just a few verses, the preacher or the listener can experience an overload of thoughts and emotions.

First, the Word is divine and thus Jesus is divine. Jesus has an intimate relationship to God witnessed throughout the entire gospel because Jesus is the Word of God become human. Coming into the world, he offers both the light of faith and not just life but eternal life to all who will respond to the offer. But no one has to respond and some reject. This also finds place in the body of the gospel.

When a person believes, that person has not the "power" to be called a child of God, but the "right." The Greek word *exousia* is better translated as "right." Faith alone offers the support for eternal life and gives to the believer the right to the title *child of God*.

Flesh carries with it the connotation of being human, but also a sacrificial tone. He pitched his tent on Earth, but then offered himself to those who believe and to God his Father. Then he returns to where he never left.

73

To understand the prologue demands an understanding of Wisdom literature in the Old Testament. God has planted an order in the universe and when a person discovers this order—what works and what does not work—that person finds happiness, contentment, fulfillment, and peace. Jesus as the Word Incarnate is wisdom incarnate. He offers the pattern to follow, which will bring happiness and fulfillment. Believing in Jesus, coming to the light he offers (the revelation of God), brings life and eternal life. The hymn does not tell how all this happens but just that it does. The gospel will fill in the unanswered questions.

The prologue also contains many references to Old Testament theology. Throughout the Old Testament God manifests certain qualities. The Hebrew words are *hesed* and *emeth*. The first cannot be translated in English by one word but has in its meaning kindness, compassion, and mercy. The second may be translated as fidelity or truth. These words come into Greek translation as *charis* and *alaetheia*, which in turn may be translated into English as grace and truth. Once the Word becomes flesh, people recognize "grace and truth," which in turn reminds the attentive reader of the qualities of God in the Old Testament. In Jesus, people will see manifest the meaning of God in the Old Testament.

The prologue tells the reader about God, humanity, and the relationship between God and humanity. In the Word Incarnate, God has entered into human history with an offer of a relationship that is none other than being a child of God. People do not have to accept the relationship. It is freely offered and freely accepted. Once accepted in faith, the child of God lives by faith, following the example of Jesus who in his daily life manifested the qualities most associated with God: kindness, compassion, mercy, and fidelity. The Gospel of John recorded his acts and his teachings. This gave to the one interested helpful hints to continue to discover the order that God planted in the universe, and thus the possibility of attaining happiness, fulfillment, contentment, and peace.

PREACHER'S PREPARATION

Very often, this gospel is not read at Christmas because most presiders prefer to use the gospel from Midnight even during the day. It is also used on the Second Sunday of Christmas. If the presider chooses to use this gospel, the emphasis could be placed on the "right" to be called children of God. Christmas often centers on children—the Christ child and then all children. Adults are also children of God. They can call God *Father* and feel secure in that relationship. As marvelous as children might be, they also are not perfect. The same is true for children of God.

Christmas is a reminder of who people are and of how they should live: dependent on God and trying to pattern their lives on the life and teachings of Jesus, living to manifest some of the qualities that God manifested in the Old Testament and Jesus manifested in the New Testament: kindness, compassion, mercy, and fidelity.

Third Sunday of Lent A

John 4:5–42

Only the Gospel of John has a mission of Jesus to Samaria. The early preaching by the followers of Jesus, however, brought many Samaritans into the early church. Geographically, Samaria lies between Galilee and Jerusalem and since Jesus often broke ordinary Jewish customs, unlike many pious Jews (many Jews would travel first east when journeying to and from Galilee) when going south, he would have willingly traveled through Samaria.

Samaritans despised Jews as Jews despised Samaritans. Samaritans accepted only the first five books of the Old Testament and intermarried with non-Jews. When they wished to help in rebuilding the Temple after the exile, the Jews returning from Babylon refused their assistance. They in turn built their temple on Mount Gerizim.

For some, this anonymous woman represented the schismatic Jews and her five husbands represent the five pagan gods they worshiped along with their commitment to the God of Israel. Also, discrimination of women was usual in both societies. Both Jews and Samaritans would have considered it improper for a man to talk to a woman in public.

The whole discussion seems theological with the woman winning at first and then, gradually, she gives way to faith until she becomes an apostle for her fellow villagers. For this unknown woman, Jesus was first an unknown traveler and then an enemy. Within the discussion, he becomes an intriguing man, then a prophet, and finally the Messiah.

On his part, Jesus has a mission to all and treats everyone alike. He meets the Samaritan woman on her own territory, engages her in a discussion, and gradually leads her to consider a commitment to both him and what he teaches. Jesus reveals himself and this enemy of the

Jews, this woman, who was also considered a sinner, accepts the offer of a relationship and becomes a follower and a preacher.

Water figures prominently. Without water, no one can live. Without the living water given by Jesus, no one can live eternally. In John 7:37–39, Jesus refers to living water, and the author clarifies by telling the reader that Jesus means the Spirit that will be given when Jesus has been glorified. Here, Jesus promises the Spirit by promising living water. The woman need only respond in faith, which she does.

Jesus also explains true worship. People will worship God in no sacred place but in and through a sacred person: Jesus. He is the one who has the Spirit, and he is the one who is the truth, revealing God. Places are not as important as people.

The disciples return confused only to see the hoard of Samaritans coming to see Jesus. Jesus is optimistic about conversions from the Samaritans, which actually happened with the early preaching by the followers of Jesus.

PREACHER'S PREPARATION

Several themes of this chapter offer opportunities for the preacher to deal with contemporary issues: the role of women in early Christianity and today; the meaning of worship; the place of church buildings; the role of the Spirit and faith within institutional Christianity; worship in and through Jesus and then in and through people.

Contrasting the Samaritan woman with Nicodemus may also help.

NICODEMUS: Male, teacher of the law, educated, respected, curious, weak defender of Jesus to the Sanhedrin, helper in the burial of Jesus. Did he ever come to faith?

SAMARITAN: Woman, outcast, sinner, curious, bold, challenger of Jesus, receptive to his teachings and then to him, woman of faith and apostle.

TEXT: Dialogue between Jesus and the Samaritan woman: as explained above.

CONTEXT: Contrast with Nicodemus; role of women in the Johannine community; faith in Jesus.

CONTEXT OF PEOPLE: Relationship between worship and daily life; or women's role in the church; or unlikely people of faith.

RESPONSE: To be determined by preacher.

Third Sunday of Lent B
John 2:13–25

Do people need more than laws and commandments or are such directions enough? The Ten Commandments of Israel offer guides for all human relationships as well as the relationship with God. Both Jews and Christians believe that if the human family lives by these commandments, the world will be at peace.

The commandments are not peculiar to Israel. Most ancient societies had similar codes of behavior, but the tradition of Israel was based on more than just practical experience. Even with these commandments, however, and in spite of it's religious tradition, Judaism was not at peace with itself and the religious experience was far from perfect. The same remains true for other religions and civilizations. Somehow, laws and commandments are not enough. They often degenerate into formal injunctions with careful outward observance but with a lack of inner acceptance.

Jesus came not to destroy the law but to fulfill it. Just to know the commandments does not mean people can fulfill them. The commandments are guidelines but are dependent upon a personal acceptance of God and others. They help but can become a burden that no one can bear. To understand the role of the commandments in the life of the Christian, followers of Jesus have to see them in the light of Jesus and his attitude and approach to life.

The gospel reading recalls the cleansing of the Temple by Jesus. The law of Judaism had developed into a complete control of life with regulations affecting every aspect of society. Specific individuals held authority, and the ordinary believer was supposed to accept this authority unquestioningly. Jesus reacted against the sterility of the religion of his day that too often was content with empty ritual and meaningless regulations. He decided to start over by restoring the house of the Lord as a house of prayer. Rules and regulations for offerings were good and necessary, but not when such rules turned the house of the Lord into a marketplace.

The Jewish authorities reacted by questioning his authority to do such a thing. Jesus replied with a double-level response. He spoke of the temple but meant the temple of his body. In Jesus, God dwells and not in a temple. The Temple may be the reminder of the presence of God but in Jesus, God is truly present. Even if people seek to destroy this presence, the reality of God in Jesus cannot be denied. The reading concludes with the remark that many believed in Jesus, but he knew what was present in the heart and had no need of further human testimony.

If Jesus came not to destroy the law but to fulfill it, if he interpreted the laws of his religion freely, in the light of love of God and neighbor, then how does the follower of Jesus react to laws and regulations?

Laws and regulations in Christianity must have their basis in the example of Jesus who was not limited to just the observance of laws. Faith in Jesus, an acceptance of him, forms the heart of the new law and only with this faith in Jesus and the love of his followers can the Christian church seek to fulfill the law of God. Relying on laws to bring about a change in people's lives brings only failure and frustration. Faith is the primary element. Knowing the Ten Commandments and trying to live them are doomed unless the believer accepts the heart of the commandments: a belief in God. Knowing God and knowing Jesus give a freedom in life that goes beyond any commandments. A person of faith fulfills the law because he/she lives under the care of God with a freedom that exceeds any effort to regulate human life. Jesus fulfilled the law in his life. Christians do likewise.

PREACHER'S PREPARATION

Today, many criticize religious education classes because they do not teach the Ten Commandments. The preacher might emphasize how Christianity is taught more by example than by words. Rules and regulations can never completely control people. Jesus seeks to persuade people, not to force them to an observance of law. Faith is the basis of Christianity and not the observance of law. The Temple was a place that reminded people of the law of God, but in Christianity Jesus and faith in him enable the followers of the Lord to actually fulfill the laws of God.

The cleansing of the Temple also points to the end of formal temple worship. Sacrificial animals and birds needed to be purchased by temple coins, which meant an exchange from the Roman coins used in Jerusalem. Both involved franchises and the clergy benefited in both cases. No money for the clergy, no animals and birds for sacrifice, meant no functioning priesthood and thus no Temple, which is what happened after AD 70.

Fourth Sunday of Lent A

John 9:1–41

Very often the Gospel of John seems like a series of one-act plays. The story of Jesus and the blind man has several scenes ending with a profession of faith by the blind man. Various characters move on and off the stage with each one or each group contributing to the overall effect. No doubt the heroes are Jesus and the blind man. Jesus throughout creates the scene in which those who witness the entire episode have to ask: "Who really sees?" and "Who is really blind?"

The play opens with Jesus and his disciples after the feast of Tabernacles. Seeing the blind man, they question: "Who sinned: the man or his parents?" In earlier times, although still present in a limited sense today, people thought that sickness was a result of a punishment by God for sin. Jesus rejects such a claim.

Throughout the Gospel of John, light and darkness form a background for many of the teachings of Jesus. The contrast of light and darkness began in the prologue and finds particular application here. Coming to the light means faith. Remaining in the darkness means a rejection of faith in Jesus. Just as earlier the author had contrasted Nicodemus with the Samaritan woman, so here the author contrasts the man born blind, supposedly in sin, with the Jewish religious leaders. Ultimately, the one who sees is the man born blind and the religious leaders are blind.

Jesus instructs the man to go to the pool of Siloam. The author explains the meaning of the word *Siloam* ("one who has been sent"). Throughout the gospel, Jesus is the one who has been sent by God. So in fact the man born blind goes to Jesus and he sees.

The next scene involves neighbors, Pharisees, and the man's parents. Throughout this passage the blind man, the sinner, takes center stage. He puts the Pharisees in their place, which causes the Pharisees to make a personal attack on him. In reality, the man born blind wins, and the Pharisees retreat by throwing him out.

Jesus reappears and the man makes his profession of faith, and the Pharisees recognize that the play has something to do with them. The man physically born blind sees with the eyes of faith. The Pharisees physically born able to see are blind.

In the time of the gospel, the narrative of the blind man reflects a historical background of the relationship between the early Christian church and the synagogue.

The reference to expelling those from the synagogue comes not from the time of Jesus, but from the time of the early church when Christianity became separated from Judaism. Both church and synagogue would have considered the opposing group unfaithful to Judaism. Each would have accused the other of blindness. Eventually, they had to go their own way and Christianity became more and more a religion of Gentiles. The question still remains: "Who sees and who is blind?"

PREACHER'S PREPARATION

Blindness can be equated with sin. The man born blind was born in sin because of his ailment, and Jesus sinned because he violated the Sabbath. Both interpretations are wrong. Jesus makes clear that the Sabbath is made for man and not vice versa, and he may freely cure on the Sabbath without offending God. The man was not a sinner because of his blindness.

God does not punish people by giving them sickness, ailments, or diseases. AIDS is not God's punishment for homosexuality. Hurricanes or earthquakes or fires are not God's wrath for abortion or any other sin. Sickness and natural disasters are part of life, and faith can help a person cope. Being blind means failing to trust in God even in the midst of human problems. The blind man was not alone. He had Jesus and with his faith he could handle any situation.

The question still remains: Who in the church today is blind and who sees?

TEXT: As explained above.

CONTEXT: Problems in early church between Christianity and Judaism and within the early church: between the Johannine community and other Christian communities.

CONTEXT OF PEOPLE: Who is blind in the church today? People, hierarchy? Maybe both. The one thought to be blind actually sees. Consideration of God, sickness, and sin.

RESPONSE: To be determined.

Fourth Sunday of Lent B

John 3:14–21

A true gift comes without strings attached. A gift symbolizes the giver and should always be given in love because of love. A gift not given in love is a bribe; a gift that expects something in return cheapens the giver; a gift given in hope that it will be used well and appreciated ennobles both the giver and the recipient. Such a gift is cherished.

God has given the gift of life and attached no strings; God gave in love because of love with the hope that all would cherish this gift. God did not demand compliance with the gift of life but surrounded life with freedom. People can do as they will, but also must learn to live with the consequences of their choices.

The gospel offers another example of God's giving. God has sent his Son as the final gift. God attaches no strings but offers Jesus as someone in whom people can believe. People need not believe; they need not pattern their lives after his example; they need not accept his teaching. God offers a gift, not a bribe. People must choose to come to the light, accept the gift of faith, and walk in the light. If some choose to remain in the darkness, that is their free choice and God will not interfere.

The author of the Gospel of John, here as in other places, reminds his readers that judgment is not reserved for a future life, meted out by God alone. People judge themselves and are already judged when they make their basic decisions. He who has come to the light, who has accepted Jesus in faith, has eternal life and need not fear any future judgment. The one who flees from the light to hide in darkness is already judged, and the future holds nothing but the ratification of that decision. Life is not a series of actions added up in the end to determine reward or punishment.

People experience basic orientations in life accepted in freedom because life is God's gift. These orientations influence the actual details of daily life. People need not wait for the end to know the outcome; they already participate in the future. Eternal life or eternal death already exists in the days, weeks, and years that comprise one single lifetime.

God gives freely; people choose freely and then live according to their choice. Living in freedom with the possibility of accepting or rejecting God can frighten. Some would like to hand over this power of decision to others, or to rules and regulations, or conduct a life that promises a just reward if carefully observed. Perhaps life would be simpler in such a process if it were possible, but if life is a personal gift, then no one can hand this gift to another to be ruled and controlled.

Finally, each person must stand in the presence of God and acknowledge just how the gift was accepted. No pope, priest, friend, book, or law can take a person's place. God will not judge, because in freedom people have judged themselves. Individuals will enter into life with God because they have always lived with God, or turn to darkness and despair because darkness and despair have already been their chosen lot.

PREACHER'S PREPARATION

The chief theme of the readings is the freedom of the individual to live as he or she chooses. God does not interfere; people shall receive what they deserve. God gives life freely; no person can control another. Every person has a basic orientation in life and lives with that basic approach. Everyone may be self-centered but should not be self-concerned. A concern for others in life foretells a concern for "the other" in dying. Deeds done according to God in life (concern for others) assure eternal life that has begun *now*.

Note: The Eastern Church, both Orthodox and Catholic, does not speak of mortal and venial sins but, rather, sins of malice and weakness. This would fit Johannine theology. Malice is living in darkness with hatred. People who come to the light in faith still commit sins of weakness but never leave the light.

Fifth Sunday of Lent A
John 11:1–45

The raising of Lazarus surely demonstrates the power of Jesus and not only stands out as a spectacular miracle but also in the Gospel of John prompted the religious authorities to seek the death of Jesus. But if Jesus performed such a miracle, many wonder why it does not appear in the other gospels. Some think that the miracle began as a parable exemplifying that Jesus gives life through death. Then the parable took on the aspects of a miracle story. The question of historicity may never be solved. The meaning, whether miracle or parable, remains the same: Jesus has power over death.

Can the dead rise and return to life? Luke records the raising of the son of the widow of Naim. Mark, Matthew, and Luke record the raising of the daughter of Jairus. The Old Testament records the raising of the dead by Elijah and Elisha, and Jesus tells his disciples to raise the dead (Matt 10:8). Evidently in the Jesus tradition, he performed such miracles. Such raisings, however, were not resurrections since in each case the individual eventually had to die and remain dead. Jesus alone rose from the dead, not to die again.

In the Gospel of John, Lazarus has been dead for three days, much different from the other raisings from the dead. The body has corrupted (John 11:39). Moreover, Lazarus was a friend of Jesus, which prompts the reaction of Martha and Mary.

The only other place in the New Testament where a Lazarus is mentioned is in the Gospel of Luke 16:19–31, a story about a poor man dying and a rich man with the poor man (Lazarus) living in the bosom of Abraham. Both Luke and John know the sisters Martha and Mary. Both stories involve death and life. Also, the parable in Luke is the only one with a proper name. Which came first: the parable of Lazarus in Luke or the story of Lazarus in John?

The Gospel of John often speaks of light and life and unbelief and belief and hearing the word of Jesus. Lazarus, who is dead and in the dark tomb, hears the word of Jesus and comes from the dark tomb and lives.

At the time of the Gospel of John, the early church faced a crisis of faith. Many thought and hoped for an imminent second coming at which time all the believers would be alive to see the triumph of Jesus. But then many followers of the Lord died and he had not returned. Some responded by pushing the second coming into the distant future. The Gospel of John takes a different approach.

Resurrection and eternal life have already begun. When a person hears the word of Jesus, believes in faith, becomes filled with the Spirit, then physical death means nothing. Resurrection is here and now (John 11:25–26). The raising of Lazarus signifies what takes place in faith. The only death that matters is the death in sin and darkness, the refusal to hear the word of Jesus and live. Martha believes (John 11:27).

The Gospel of John, however, and this chapter, does not deny some future fulfillment and a final resurrection. What the author seems to want is for people to pay attention to what has already taken place. Jesus has already given life. For those who believe, they need not fear death or judgment for "he who hears my word and believes in him who sent me has eternal life" (John 5:24).

PREACHER'S PREPARATION

Very often Christianity has been accused of emphasizing the future life so much that followers of Jesus pay little attention to the present life. Thus, Marx called religion the opiate of the people. "Suffer now and enjoy it later" has been the leitmotiv of many preachers. The Gospel of John rejects this approach to Christianity. Jesus has already given life to those who believe.

Life on Earth is to be enjoyed because it has been blessed by God through Jesus. Life now has a value and a purpose and a goodness. Concentrate on what has already happened in faith. Do not worry about death and judgment for the believer has already come to the light, has already begun to enjoy the happiness of being a child of God. Salvation is *now*, so enjoy it.

Fifth Sunday of Lent B
John 12:20–33

Where is love? What is life's purpose? What does life mean? When a person asks these questions, he or she faces adulthood and maturity. The rich young man of the gospels went to Jesus when he was troubled with the meaning of life, and Jesus told him to lose his life for the sake of finding it. Give up all and follow Jesus if you wish to find the answer to the riddle of life.

Sunday's gospel goes further and talks about the grain of wheat falling into the ground and dying to bring forth fruit. The author writes of loving life to discover that it is lost and hating life to find it. What does it mean to die, to lose one's life, to hate one's life?

The Word of God implies that if people are interested in finding meaning and purpose in life, then they must be willing to overcome any selfishness and pride and freely give of self to Jesus and his gospel. They need to move from being completely self-centered to being other-concerned.

For the contemporary believer who reads or hears these words in the liturgy, the meaning of finding life in death may be difficult to understand and more difficult to relate to one's personal life. To die to oneself means to share in the sacrifice of Jesus, who died to his own will in his acceptance of the will of God his Father, and who died to himself in his faithful love of others. If the grain of wheat, personal lives, must die, then this involves an acceptance of the will of God and a living for the sake of others.

In the past, Roman Catholics found it somewhat easy to discover the will of God since it was identified with church law and practice, as well as with the commands of those who were leaders in the church. Today, people might find it more difficult to discover the will of God. The ascetical practices that characterized much of Roman Catholic tradition have fallen by the wayside. Even the pope and bishops seem reluctant to identify themselves so easily with the will of God. What was once easy to know has become harder to discover today.

Three aids, however, can be used in the believer's effort to understand the discovery of self through the giving of one's life. First, prayer is necessary. People must be aware of the presence of God in their lives and give room for the Holy Spirit. To die to oneself means to make room in life for God. Prayer is part of that room.

Second, Jesus gave his life for his friends and his enemies. The crucifixion alone should not be seen as the sacrifice of Jesus; Calvary was the culmination, the supreme manifestation of how he lived. When he died, he died after he had lived a life of doing good to all. "He went about doing good" (Acts 10:38).

To die to self, to share in the sacrifice of Jesus, to be filled with the Spirit mean to open oneself to others. To be kind and gracious and helpful and considerate even when people are not like that causes a dying. Service offered causes pain since it is offered at the expense of the giver.

Third, Roman Catholics maintain a strong ascetical tradition of sharing with those who are in need. Unfortunately, in contemporary society sharing is often limited to the giving of alms. People can also give of time or talents and share each other's burdens.

"He who loses his life will find it." Life comes through dying for self, but too often people are afraid to give room to God for fear of losing what they already have. If only people would overcome fear and open themselves to share in the sacrifice of Jesus, they would learn by experience that dying for the sake of God and others is to find life.

PREACHER'S PREPARATION

The homilist might concentrate on ascetical practices. People need not spend hours in prayer, nor can work be the only prayer. The homilist might also develop the theme of sharing time and talents. The end of Lent is approaching. What have you done for your mind, your body, and your soul?

Note: Repentance means to rethink. In the beginning of Lent people are supposed to do some rethinking on how they are living. This should include practices that benefit the mind, the body, and the soul as well as almsgiving and prayer. Just before Holy Week is a good time to do an examination of conscience on Lenten practices, which could be the response offered by the homilist.

Fifth Sunday of Lent C

John 8:1–11

For many reasons, the account of Jesus with the woman taken in adultery has been universally accepted as not belonging in the Gospel of John. Over the centuries it has appeared also in manuscripts within the Gospel of Luke. Evidently, ancient scribes wanted to preserve the story but did not know where to place it. It sounds more like a Synoptic story than belonging to the Gospel of John. Nevertheless, it ended up in the Gospel of John probably because most copyists thought it caused less disturbance here than anywhere else.

The story has several settings. It begins with a crowd and Jesus, shifts to Scribes and Pharisees confronting Jesus along with the woman, and then the roles are reversed as Jesus confronts the Scribes and Pharisees and, finally, just the woman and Jesus remain.

The woman has been caught in the act of adultery, and the Scribes and Pharisees bring her to Jesus, but themselves seem to have little concern for her. They want to deal with Jesus. They know what Moses would do so now what will Jesus do? Will he contradict the Law of Moses and thus separate himself from the Mosaic tradition, or will he contradict himself and his teachings on mercy and forgiveness? They are not interested in the fate of the woman or even the injured husband who is never mentioned. They want to bring a charge against Jesus (John 8:6a).

Jesus reverses roles and challenges them. Over the centuries some have conjectured that Jesus wrote on the ground the secret sins of those present. The text offers no support for this theory. It seems rather that Jesus appears disinterested and merely doodles on the ground. Then he gets up and continues the dialogue. The implication is that all have committed sexual sins. Gradually, the Scribes and Pharisees drift away and possibly the crowds as well, leaving Jesus alone with the woman.

92

Augustine remarks: "Only two remain: the wretched woman and the incarnation of mercy."

Jesus alone addresses the woman, and the words have nothing to do with her sin but rather her accusers. Jesus also uses "you." The woman is no longer an object of revilement and condemnation but a dialogue partner with Jesus. The woman calls Jesus *Lord*, out of reverence and respect. Since no one condemns her, Jesus offers her a new way of life and unconditionally and on his own authority forgives the woman. Also by his actions, he does not follow the Law of Moses, which would have called for her being stoned to death. The story may not belong in the Gospel of John, but it exemplifies a characteristic of Jesus in this gospel: "And the word became flesh and dwelt among us full of grace and truth" (John 1: 14). Jesus manifests the kindness, compassion, mercy, and faithfulness of God to sinners.

PREACHER'S PREPARATION

The preacher might briefly introduce some of the questions associated with the study of scripture and the transmission of manuscripts. The Word of God has been communicated humanly with all the limitations of what humans do.

The story demonstrates mercy and forgiveness as well as pride and haughtiness on the part of Scribes and Pharisees. Sexual sins may be sins of malice but most often involve weakness. The question remains: "Who has not committed some sexual sin, if not in action, in thought?" They are not the greatest sins nor do they exclude from the kingdom. Sexuality needs to be integrated into the human person. When it is not, then sins occur. Sexual sins demand a crossing of desire and opportunity. They are best controlled by avoiding this intersection.

The fathers of the church often used the story of the woman taken in adultery to symbolize the church with all its failings and sins. In the end, Jesus will not condemn his bride in spite of all her sins. The church has done much good even as it needs constantly to be reformed.

Holy Thursday
John 13:1–15

In the Jewish celebration of the Passover Seder, the youngest member of the family asks: "Why is this night different than all the others?" Christians could ask the same question when they gather to celebrate the Holy Thursday Mass. This is the night it all began. This is when Jesus gathered with his disciples to celebrate a farewell meal the night before he died. This is the night when he blessed and broke bread, and blessed and shared a cup of wine with the instruction: "Do this in memory of me."

The Jewish Passover recalls how God was good to the Jewish people in the past, and they pray that God will be good to them in the present and in the future. The first reading for Holy Thursday narrates the first Passover experience. Christians on Holy Thursday recall when God was good to them in the past in the life and death of Jesus. They experience now the presence of God and grace, and they look forward to future glory.

The Gospel of John has the longest section on the Last Supper yet does not narrate the story of the Eucharist. Where one might expect to read about the Eucharist, this gospel narrates Jesus washing the feet of his disciples. For some, this might seem strange. On examining the foot washing, comparing it with the crucifixion and then with the Eucharist, something in common becomes evident: Jesus is present to his friends when they are in need; he offers himself and they are changed.

When Jesus washes the feet of his disciples, he performs a menial task usually performed by slaves or servants. He offers himself to them in this action and they become better: They share in his inheritance and then should minister to each other.

On Calvary Jesus joins the fate of all humans. He accepts death since all must die. He offers himself to God with confidence, and human history is changed. Redemption and salvation have taken place for all. The value, the worth, and the dignity of every human being (redemption) Jesus preserves. He has redeemed people. And even in a cruel death, God is present to all who trust in God.

In the Eucharist, Jesus is present to his friends, offers himself as food and drink, and those who receive him are joined to God through the gift of Jesus. In the Eucharist, the followers of Jesus receive a pledge of God's continuing presence in their lives and wish each other peace. They become better people.

Jesus warned his followers: "In the world you will have trouble, but have a light heart; I have overcome the world" (John 16:33). In the celebration of Holy Thursday, Christians recall how God was good to them in the past and will be good to them *now* and in the future for God has given them Jesus. "If God has given us his son, is there anything God will deny us?" (Rom 8:32).

Holy Thursday gives hope for the future. Christians know Jesus remains with them in the Eucharist. People are already redeemed. Their value, worth, and dignity can never be destroyed for Jesus has said so. People have experienced the positive presence of God (salvation) in the past and in the present, and will continue to experience the saving presence of God in the future forever. Christians can remain of good cheer, with a light heart, for the Lord Jesus has overcome the world.

PREACHER'S PREPARATION

The homilist might emphasize how the liturgy recalls the past, celebrates the present, and looks forward to the future. The ancient hymn, *O Sacrum Convivium*, contains these elements and could form a context for the homily: "O holy coming together in which Christ is received, his passion is recalled, the person is filled with grace, and the pledge of future glory is given."

The relationship between the foot washing, the passion, and the Eucharist in the Gospel of John could also form a fitting conclusion. The liturgy recalls what Jesus did in the past, what he does for the church today, and what he promises for the future.

TEXT: As explained above.

CONTEXT: Night before he died, foot washing takes the place of Eucharist.

CONTEXT OF CONGREGATION: Need to recall experiences of God through Jesus in the past; need to believe in redemption: value, worth, and dignity.

RESPONSE: Celebrate life as gift from God through Jesus.

Good Friday
John 18:1—19:42

Usually when people think of Good Friday, they think about pain, sorrow, and the agony and death of Jesus. For more than twelve hundred years, however, the church has read the passion according to John on Good Friday. In this gospel, Jesus experiences no pain or suffering. The way of the cross is a triumphant parade.

The Gospel of John has no agony in the garden and no pain. Jesus acts in control at all times and even tells his captors what they must do. When he proclaims that "I am" (a substitute for the name of God in Hebrew), they all fall down in an appropriate gesture in the presence of the divine. Jesus needs no one to help him carry the cross. On the cross, Jesus reigns with a concern for his mother. And his mother together with the Beloved Disciple, the two perfect disciples, receive his Spirit. He proclaims "it is finished." Jesus has accomplished redemption for the human race.

Throughout this gospel, Jesus reveals God as compassionate, merciful, kind, and faithful. Jesus has lived and will die as the human face of God. Redemption is accomplished. The value, worth, dignity given to every human being by being created in the image and likeness of God will never be destroyed. Even if individuals try to destroy this gift of God, Jesus has seen to it that this value will never be lost or destroyed.

In Jesus, people have experienced the saving presence of God. God has entered into human history in the life and ministry of Jesus and now, as he dies, he manifests how God can be present in every human dying even a cruel death.

Good Friday celebrates the triumph of goodness over evil. When people try to destroy what is good, God intervenes and will not allow it. The human family tried to say "no" to goodness by bringing Jesus to

Calvary, but God has said "yes" to the power of goodness in Jesus and so Jesus reigns in death, which issues in the resurrection.

In the midst of a sad and often painful world, Jesus always gives to his followers a reason to rejoice. People experience the presence of God in the thousand ways life is made more pleasant. Moments of salvation take place when winter gives way to spring as the world takes on a newness that lightens the step of everyone. When people send a thank-you note or flowers, make a telephone call, or visit a sick person, each becomes a moment when God becomes present in life through the kindness of others.

Good Friday accomplished redemption and salvation, and thus in the Gospel of John, pain and suffering submerge in the joy and happiness of God's saving presence. Jesus has thirsted for people to experience God's presence. Jesus has fulfilled a ministry in which people have seen, observed, and experienced forgiveness, compassion, kindness, and fidelity. Calvary has made salvation and redemption possible. Now people not only must acknowledge how they have experienced the goodness of God, but must in turn offer to others what they have experienced.

Good Friday should not be a day of mourning. People should have done that on Palm Sunday. With the Gospel of John read during the Good Friday service, this should be a day of rejoicing in what God has done for the human race through Jesus, including his death. Since Jesus has made salvation possible for all, people, especially followers of Jesus, should contribute to moments of salvation in each other's lives. The glorious parade to Calvary in the Gospel of John has led to the life-giving death of Jesus, who then gave the Spirit to his perfect disciples, his mother and the Beloved Disciple. Rejoice. Good Friday is here!

PREACHER'S PREPARATION

The homilist might concentrate on the special aspects of the passion according to John. The author offers neither pain nor suffering. Jesus reigns gloriously from the cross. He is always under complete control and accomplished redemption for all. Jesus assured that the God-given goodness to all people can never be destroyed by any amount of evil.

The perfect believers stood at the base of the cross, the Mother of Jesus and the Beloved Disciple. They received his Spirit for all.

TEXT: As explained above.

CONTEXT OF TEXT: The glorious Jesus in the gospel of John; no pain or suffering; always in control. Redemption and salvation *now*.

CONTEXT OF PEOPLE: Sadness, guilt do not belong on Good Friday.

RESPONSE: Think of what you have been given; offer moments of salvation to others.

Easter Sunday

John 20:1–9

Easter, like spring, celebrates life, rebirth, hope, and joy. Jesus lives; he is risen, living among us. Jesus did not suffer the fate of all humankind in dying to remain the dead savior; he is risen. This faith Christians celebrate, giving hope each spring.

The resurrection of Jesus makes him different from any other person. His resurrection makes believers different as well. No longer must people remain suspended between hope and despair, darkness and light. The one like us in all things but sin has been the faithful and loving Son of God; as a result, the human race and all creation are blessed and given hope. The God who created all people has entered into history and has shown his face in Jesus. That face is loving and forgiving.

The church has always preached the same good news. Christians believe that Jesus is risen and his followers are Easter people. The resurrection drives out all gloom and fills life with joy and expectation that will bind the days into years and the years into a lifetime.

The gospel reading from John begins the resurrection appearances. Peter and John run to the tomb after hearing the testimony of Mary and believe that Jesus is risen. In some ways the Fourth Gospel is the gospel least interested in the resurrection of Jesus. For John, the death of Jesus is the hour of his exaltation and glorification. When Jesus died he poured forth his Spirit (John 19:30) to renew the Earth. Death, resurrection, ascension, and Pentecost are all telescoped into the event of the crucifixion and glorification.

When John does treat the appearances of the Risen Lord, he has a distinct purpose. In each case, the disciples are troubled and confused. Jesus was glorified in his death, and in his resurrection he returns to give birth to faith and to encourage and to aid his followers. Now that Jesus was risen, people could understand that by living and dying like all people, Jesus made it possible for all to live a good human life and die a human death supported and comforted by the presence of God.

An additional note from the Fourth Gospel that should be appreciated is that Jesus responded to the needs of his followers. Mary was disconsolate and felt alone; Thomas had his doubts; the disciples labored and caught nothing in their fishing boats. In each case Jesus was present and responded to their needs.

On Easter, Christians gather as a community to profess their faith, and all are aware of how much this faith needs to grow and become stronger. On Easter, believers can turn to the Risen Lord and ask for a deepening of that faith, being assured that Jesus is present to his friends when they are in need. Jesus is alive today as he was with the disciples on the first Easter.

Christians listen to the Word and celebrate the presence of Jesus in the Eucharist. In a troubled world, in the midst of a personal life that is mixed with joy and sorrow, the presence of Jesus is healing and consoling. All have great reason to say: Jesus is alive. *Happy Easter!*

PREACHER'S PREPARATION

On great feasts, preachers really do not have to say too much. The feast itself and the readings speak more eloquently than most preachers. I would suggest that the homily be brief and concentrate on the meaning of Easter as a sign of hope, just as spring is filled with hope, and the notion that the Risen Lord is always present to his friends when they are in need.

Second Sunday
of Easter A–B–C
John 20:19–31

The forgiveness of sins causes some concern for Christians. All believe that God forgives, but how is forgiveness related to the Catholic tradition of the sacrament of penance? All believe that through the ministry of the church in the sacrament of penance they are reconciled to God through Jesus, but is this necessary, or are other ways of being reconciled possible? Surely people can be forgiven by asking God to forgive; then what is the value of the sacrament of reconciliation or penance?

The Gospel of John places that forgiveness of sins within the context of an Easter appearance of Jesus. The disciples are gathered in the upper room for fear of the Jews. In all likelihood they are also frightened because they have heard that Jesus is risen; he is alive and was seen by friends. What will he say to them? Conscious of their sins, they knew their failure to remain faithful to the Lord in his passion. During his ministry, they had protested that they were ready to die for him, but when the moment of decision arrived, they fled (except for some women and the Beloved Disciple) and left him alone to face his unjust death.

Will Jesus condemn his disciples for their sins? Will he mock them for their false boasting and overbearing pride? Will he demand some penance on their part before he will treat them again as his friends?

Jesus comes into their midst and wishes them peace. He does it twice, and then he speaks of the forgiveness of sins that will be the ministry of the community. Peace or *shalom* in Hebrew is the greeting that expresses all that is good. It is a prayer for prosperity, for friends, for family, for a long life, for God's blessing. All that is good, noble, true, lovely, and Godlike is expressed in the greeting of peace. The one who offers the greeting extends a loving offer of all good things.

To a group of sinful followers, Jesus offers the greeting of peace. All is forgotten; he harbors no ill will for his weak followers. He does not incriminate or condemn; Jesus does not even mock or remind them of their weakness. As they are aware of their sins and receive forgiveness, so his followers must offer this same forgiveness to others.

To understand the meaning of forgiveness of sins in the Christian community, this context of human failure and divine forgiveness seems essential. God is not a vengeful God demanding the pound of flesh. God knows human weakness and offers forgiveness and reconciliation to all who seek to be reconciled in peace. God does not bargain; God does not lay unbearable burdens on the back of the sinner; God, through Jesus and his church, offers the gift and promise of peace.

The choice of words in the gospel is also important for understanding the sacrament. John uses the Greek *mathetai*, which means disciples and not necessarily the twelve apostles, the leaders of the community. The gift of forgiveness and the responsibility of reconciliation are given first to the church in the Fourth Gospel and not primarily to the leaders of the community. The whole church has the task to bring forgiveness and reconciliation, not just church leaders. Sinners belong to the community, and the community must offer forgiveness to one another. If God forgives and reconciles, so individual members must forgive and be ministers of reconciliation. The forgiveness of a sinner belongs to the community, just as the sinner must seek the pardon of the community. In all, the context of the Gospel of John creates the atmosphere of the sacrament: in the midst of human sin and failure, Jesus offers the gift of peace.

PREACHER'S PREPARATION

The theme of the homily, if based on the gospel, should be the sacrament of penance. With the new rite of Penance, the relationship of the sacrament to the church is more evident. This Sunday would be an ideal time to bring in this communal element of the sacrament. It also could be a time to explain the ritual.

Note: Recall the terminology of the Eastern Churches: sins of malice and weakness. Recall also that in the Catholic tradition the very celebration of the Eucharist is the experience of the forgiveness of sins. Some will say that this should involve only venial sins, but this becomes a moot point when considering sins of malice and weakness.

Third Sunday of Easter C
John 21:1–19

Authority these days seems to have its troubles. Many question political, parental, and even religious authority. Some will even talk about a crisis in authority, and there seems to be a good foundation for such a statement. The loss of authority in every area, especially in the religious domain, often causes great concern for all members of a church.

The church as part of society is often affected by the turmoil and problems of the more general society. If the church is Jesus existing in a real world, then the environment of the world affects the church. If society is troubled, then the church will feel the effects of the anxiety.

Historically, however, there have been additional problems with authority in the church. Too often, the role of authority in the Christian community has been so affected by the prevailing image of authority of society that the exercise of church authority took on the trappings and the mode of exercise of civil authority.

In the Middle Ages, the authority of the pope and bishops was often modeled after the authority of kings and princes. Religious orders that came into existence in the seventeenth century appear to be modeled after the political despotism of seventeenth-century Europe. Those that were founded earlier in the Middle Ages are more democratic, reflecting the more lenient type of political regime. At this point some may ask: What does all this have to do with the scripture readings?

The gospel reading is the final chapter of John. The historical context is a troubled community that must come to grips with church authority and the developing hierarchical church. The Johannine community will not deny the authority given to Peter and exercised by leaders who have inherited their authority in the church from Peter, but will place the authority of Peter within its proper context. In so doing, the gospel also places the role of all authority in the church in its proper context.

Peter is asked three times if he loves Jesus. Only when he responds repeatedly that he does can he have a share in the pastoral office of ministry in the church of Jesus. This is the first criterion. Jesus goes further and insists that for Peter to exercise a share of his authority, he has to be willing to die for Jesus. Just as the Good Shepherd will die for one of the flock, so Peter will have to do the same. To love Jesus fervently and to die for him and thus for his flock establish authority in the church. If an individual aspires to a role of leadership in the Christian church, then that person has to fulfill the criterion as given in the Gospel of John.

The comparison of this exercise of authority with the more traditional manifestation of authority in the church is evident. Historically, too often the criterion of church authority was forgotten and, instead, the church was influenced by the prevailing exercise of political authority. If there is a crisis of authority in the church today, the only possible resolution lies in the return to the biblical understanding of authority: love of Jesus and a willingness to die for him.

Some may wonder what this means to the average Roman Catholic who sits in the pew on Sunday and has little to say about the way authority is exercised. Thomas Jefferson once remarked that people get the type of leadership they deserve. If believers insist on a type of leadership that is based on the love of Jesus, then the community will give birth to such authority. If the community settles for anything else, then it has no one to blame but itself.

Christians celebrate the presence of the Lord in the community by word and sacrament. If faith means anything, that word and sacrament will give all believers the courage to purify the community by insisting on the effective leadership that is modeled on the Good Shepherd, who gave his life willingly for his sheep.

PREACHER'S PREPARATION

The homily could center on the meaning of authority in the church. It is not the same as civil authority. In reality, the only authority is that of Jesus and the Spirit. At the same time, the church needs some organization, and that will demand obedience and the exercise of authority.

The preacher could take the occasion to exhort the people to accept their role in making sure that authority is exercised well on their behalf. This would include a true critique of bishop, pastor, assistants, and so on. The homily should also stress the need for church authority to continue to function in an often sinful world.

Fourth Sunday of Easter

A — *John 10:1–10*

B — *John 10:11–18*

C — *John 10:27–30*

The Gospel of John contains only two parables, the parable of the good shepherd in chapter 10 that is really two (the door and the shepherd), and in chapter 15 the parable of the vine and the branches. Since all admit that Jesus spoke in parables and the Synoptic Gospels have many, if John chose only two, they must have great importance both for the community and for the gospel. The Fourth Sunday of the Easter cycle presents chapter 10 in its entirety over the three years. It seems better to deal with the entire chapter and then the preacher can decide what to emphasize in each year.

The two parables concern the shepherd (John: 3b–5) and the door or gate (John 1–3a). They interrelate but offer different aspects of the relationship between Jesus and his followers. Jesus as the door or gate has two meanings. He is the gate and through him alone is the proper way to approach the sheep. He is also the shepherd. The reaction to the parables is failure to understand (John 10:6).

Then the author explains the gate (John 10:7–10). Those who enter through Jesus (faith) experience salvation and have life abundantly. The door brings security for the sheep and protection. As Jesus himself protects his sheep, Jesus as the door will guard them.

The Old Testament also has the image of God as the shepherd (Ezek 34:11ff. and Isa 40: 11). For an agrarian society, the parable makes much sense. Even people today can understand the need for nourishment, security, and guidance, and people, like sheep, need all of these.

If the author of the Gospel of John chose this as the first of the parables, then the meaning behind it must have special significance and must fit into his theology. A parable is a simple comparison taken from ordinary life with sufficient vividness and strangeness, "leaving the mind in sufficient doubt to tease it into active thought" (C. H. Dodd, *Parables of the Kingdom*, New York: Scribners, 1961, p. 34). All parables do just that. This one from John should cause even twenty-first-century urban Christians to do some thinking.

The Gospel of John emphasizes relationships. It is filled with individuals who relate to Jesus by faith or by rejection. When the sheep hear the voice of the shepherd, they respond in faith, trusting the shepherd and following him. They have very little to do to find nourishment and protection. Faith in Jesus is the basis of Christianity. The author of this gospel stresses the essential elements of what it means to be a Christian and that means faith in Jesus. Here it is not so much believing in what Jesus says, but, rather, in trusting him and following.

Jesus is also the Good Shepherd. Christians live as members of a community but are never lost in the crowd. The Good Shepherd, the noble shepherd, the model shepherd, gives security, rest, and nourishment. Jesus knows his flock as individuals. He calls each by name, and each in turn responds to that voice. The Gospel of John teaches that all have a personal relationship with the Lord. Jesus does not confuse someone with anyone else. When believers respond in faith to the Lord, they have the actual experience and not just the promise of eternal life.

The imagery is pastoral and far removed from the scene of a contemporary American city, but the theme behind the image is more than just familiar. People feel good and important when someone calls them by name. When a person loves another, one responds with joy at the very sound of the person's voice. When in the presence of a friend one loves dearly, the human heart beats quickly with expectation and happiness. The Good Shepherd never confuses any of his sheep, never forgets the person, and never abandons those who love him. Instead, he delights in the presence of his beloved, even to the point of giving up his life for his loved one.

Jesus as the Good Shepherd asks a personal response to him in faith. Believe in him and in his Word; trust in him for all your needs; be assured that you are never abandoned and overlooked or alone. Have confidence that your life is so precious in his eyes that Jesus gladly would give up his own life. This is the message of the Good Shepherd.

No doubt, in this passage the author presents a rather rigid individualism. It is a question of "Jesus and me" living in faith and benefiting from the love of Jesus. At the same time in this section of the gospel, some presence of the larger community persists since the imagery is that of a flock. To try to reconcile the ideas of individualism and the community, all need to recognize that at the root of Christian faith and Christian community is the personal response to Jesus as revealer and mediator of God's love to humanity. Without this personal acceptance of Jesus in the life of the individual, no faith will survive and no one can ever experience any sense of a true community.

To be God's children, to be part of God's family, presupposes this relationship to Jesus. To be saved means that the individual has found room in his or her heart for the presence of Jesus. It also means to experience the peace, happiness, and contentment of acknowledging the reign of God in the acceptance of the Gospel of Jesus. Just because a person has grown up with Jesus does not necessarily mean that the person has accepted him, and even an initial acceptance must be renewed.

God gives no clear blueprint in life for anyone. Believers trust in God and in the Son who gives light to even the darkest moment. The voice of the Good Shepherd is heard today in the land as it was heard in Palestine. If only people would harken to his voice!

PREACHER'S PREPARATION

The theme of the Good Shepherd offers a host of ideas for the homilist: Jesus' awareness of his sheep; his ability to call each by name without confusion; the sense of protection that Jesus offers; the call to listen to his voice; the sense of feeding and giving comfort. The homilist can use all of the above themes to help the congregation to be aware of the great love of God and love of Jesus for them as individuals. There is no great emphasis on the relationship of the sheep to one another, only the relationship to Jesus.

Just because a person has grown up with Jesus does not mean that person has accepted Jesus in faith. Doors are important. When closed, a person is excluded if he or she is outside. If inside, the person is secure. Jesus is an open door first, and the person goes through that door by faith and then security follows. Jesus calls each person by name. This alone brings a sense of self-worth and importance. Parents often call their children by each other's names. Jesus never does that. The nourishment comes by his teachings and by his presence. The good sheep trust Jesus now and in the future since his purpose in coming was to give life abundantly.

The Easter season is a season of hope, just as springtime is the time of hope and new life. The follower of Jesus can feel confident in the present and in the future.

Fifth Sunday of Easter A

John 14:1–12

The farewell discourses of the Gospel of John, running from chapters 13 to 17, all take place at the Last Supper. They are plural, since it seems that the author has joined several speeches of Jesus together. Most people are familiar with the thirteenth chapter or at least with the washing of the feet that begins it.

The fourteenth chapter, parts that can be found in the Sundays after Easter in Cycles A and C, offers particular theology coming from the Johannine community, as well as from the ministry of Jesus. The chapter itself could be separated from the rest of them in this section and make perfect sense.

Jesus begins with promises. First, he will bring his disciples home (John 14:1–4). Here he uses traditional eschatology with spatial images, but then tells them that such imagery is inadequate. Jesus himself is the place of divine glory.

In the Old Testament tradition, the glory of God is the manifestation of God's power and goodness. The greatest glory of God in the Old Testament was God's glory in the Exodus, which created the people of Israel. Then the power of God competed with the power of Pharaoh and God won. The goodness of God becomes evident since God takes a captive people, sets them free, and gives them land.

The actual resurrection of Jesus manifests God's glory since God has power over death, and God refuses to allow the goodness of Jesus to be destroyed. Jesus as risen becomes the glory of God manifested to all who will believe.

To share in the glory of God, no journey is necessary. Jesus himself is the way. He is the truth that reveals God and the life promised to all who believe. Philip listens but does not understand, and so Jesus declares his relationship to God: "Whoever sees me has seen the Father."

Jesus is the human face of God. If people want to know something about God, they have only to look at Jesus. Observe how he lived and died; listen to what he has to say and share in that relationship to God by living as Jesus did.

To make clear this relationship, Jesus explains further. Where Jesus is, the Father is; what Jesus speaks, he has learned from God. What he does, God does through him. And so believe.

If the disciples believe, then they will do what Jesus has done. The disciple becomes God's human face to others. The entire Gospel of John returns again and again to its beginning. In the prologue, Jesus gives to those who believe the right to be called children of God. Then, as Jesus manifested the qualities of God: kindness, compassion, mercy, and fidelity, so the disciples will share in the glory of God by living these same virtues.

PREACHER'S PREPARATION

Everyone has images of God. Some see God as the Creator, judge, or evaluator. If Jesus is the human face of God, however valuable these other images may be, they pale in relationship to the true image of God seen in Jesus.

A compassionate person enters into the experience of another. If the experience is good, it is doubly enjoyed; if sad, the person bearing the pain has assistance. The kind person emphasizes what is positive. The mean person concentrates on the negative. Mercy is self-evident, and fidelity means remaining true in the midst of infidelity.

Followers of Jesus already share in the glory of God by their commitment to Jesus in faith. They take a lifetime in living the virtues associated with Jesus and thus with God. The preacher might first deal with the various images of God, and then concentrate on the declaration that Jesus is the human face of God. The response expected of the congregation might be to take one of those virtues and live it just for the day.

TEXT: As explained above.

CONTEXT: Johannine theology of Jesus as the human face of God.

CONTEXT OF THE CONGREGATION: How can a believer continue the mission of Jesus?

RESPONSE: Choose one of the divine virtues, and practice it for a day or two or more.

Fifth Sunday of Easter B

John 15:1–8

The season after Easter emphasizes the relationship that Christians should have to Jesus as Risen Lord and the effects of faith on ordinary living. The parable of the good shepherd stressed the individual relationship to Jesus, and the parable of the vine and the branches has a similar meaning.

At first sight, some might think that Jesus is talking about the community aspects of Christianity and his church when he chooses as his parable the vine and the branches. On closer examination, however, it seems that he talks again about its personal relationship to himself.

Jesus is the vine and the individual branches have life and bear the fruit of love only if they remain in relationship with him. The parable shows no concern for a relationship between or among the branches. If some branches are pruned, if some wither and are burned, such events have little effect on the other branches. Jesus calls upon the individual to remain in him and live by him even if some others fall away. The individual must maintain his or her personal relationship to Jesus and bear the fruit of love. Jesus then promised life and glory given by the Father. A branch must stay close to Jesus and live. Move away from Jesus and the branch will die.

Faith remains primary. The Gospel of John records only the commandment of love of the brethren, but the gospel is also filled with references to individual faith in Jesus. The follower of Jesus believes and loves and so Jesus remains with the follower through the power of his Spirit. The increasing consolation of the Spirit of Jesus in the life of the believer gave the early Christians the enthusiasm as well as the courage to live and die as heralds of the Gospel of the Lord.

The acceptance of Jesus is not a once-and-for-all decision. Faith in Jesus does not always imply a stunning conversion as experienced by

Paul, and it may not involve a precise moment in time. The early followers of Jesus accepted him in faith, allowed him and his gospel to
influence their lives, and from this commitment came the love of the
brethren.

Do the contemporary followers of Jesus continue to make that
commitment in faith? Do they love one another? These are questions
individuals must ask themselves. To believe in Jesus means to live
according to his gospel, which involves a practical love of the brethren.
No person does this at one moment in life, but must continually reaf-
firm that faith commitment and continually struggle to practice an
effective faith by a love of all believers. Easter reminds all of faith in the
Risen Lord and encourages all to propel that faith to its natural outcome: the love of the brethren.

Sometimes critics of the Gospel of John call attention to the type
of exclusive love expected. The members of the community do not have
to love enemies but only the brethren, the members of the community.
The thought behind the love command may signify how difficult it is to
love those who are distant, either physically or psychologically, unless
one loves those who are close. Begin to love those near and dear, and
then the possibility of loving even enemies might happen.

PREACHER'S PREPARATION

The point of the gospel is related to last week's gospel. The two
parables of the good shepherd and the vine and the branches are concerned with a personal relationship to Jesus in faith. The latter concludes this with the injunction to bear fruit that is explained as a love of
the brethren.

Faith and love make the church. Without both elements there can
be no effective Christianity.

Fifth Sunday of Easter C
John 13:31–35

The thirteenth chapter of John begins the series of talks by Jesus known as the farewell discourses. It appears to be a series since some of the chapters seem independent of each other. Chapter 14 ends with "Rise, let us go hence," and then chapter 15 begins anew. Chapter 17 also seems like an independent talk by Jesus. All of them take place at the Last Supper in the Gospel of John.

The beginning of this chapter is well known since it narrates the washing of the feet by Jesus. The announcement of the betrayal follows, and Judas completes the process of separation when he leaves the upper room. The author remarks: "And it was night." The betrayer goes into the darkness. Now Jesus speaks to his closest followers, giving them a new commandment.

The chapter begins with Jesus gathered with others, but no title is given to those who are present with him until verse 22. When Jesus has announced that one of them will betray him, the author says the "disciples" looked at one another. Nowhere in the Gospel of John does the author use the title *apostle*. He uses the title *the Twelve* four times, each time in a negative context (John 6: 67, 70, 71; 20:24). This gospel uses the title *disciple*, follower, or student, which in the New Testament has the broadest connotation. It means anyone who follows Jesus, men or women—those part of the inner circle and the more general group who have come to believe. At the Last Supper "disciples" were present.

Jesus' commandment of love forms the central teaching of Jesus. Here in this gospel, however, it takes on a different tone. The love of God and neighbor is not new to Jesus or to Christianity. The Old Testament has such a teaching, and Jesus quotes Deuteronomy 6:4 and Leviticus 19:18 when asked about the great commandments (Mark 12:29–31; Matt 22:37–40; Luke 10:26–27).

In the Gospel of John, however, Jesus has only one commandment of love and that is the love of the brethren. This same theme appears in 1 John 4:11. For this author the love of God cannot exist without the primary love of the brethren.

This gospel also does not expect the love of enemies. Love begins with members of the faith community. How can one ever hope to love those far and outside unless that person has love for those who are close and within?

Jesus gives the measure by which the brethren, the "disciples," must love each other: as Jesus did. This means a willingness to die for those who share the same faith in Jesus. Every member of the Christian community should be willing to die for any other member, and every member of the community should know that anyone would die for him or for her. Such is the new commandment.

PREACHER'S PREPARATION

As difficult as it may seem, the homilist should concentrate on the love that should exist within the Christian community. Too often Christians take those nearest and dearest to them for granted. How can one ever hope to love and care for others if first that person does not love and care for those near and dear? Very often it is easier to try to love enemies since one need not deal with them all of the time. How realistic is it to believe that any member of the community would die for any other member of the community? Yet, that is the measure Jesus gives his followers by which they are to evaluate their love.

Perhaps Christians can begin to try to measure up by at least recognizing the talents in every member, and doing whatever is possible for all members of the community to use and develop those talents. And those with special talents could use them for the benefit of the whole community.

Sixth Sunday of Easter
A — *John 14:15–21*
C — *John 14:23–29*

This section of the Gospel of John contains the most significant references to the Spirit. This does not mean that the Spirit is not part of the earlier sections. In the very first chapter, the author proclaims that the Spirit descended and remained on Jesus (John 1:32). In the third chapter, God gives the Spirit fully (John 3:34). Jesus also baptizes in the Spirit (John 1:32). In this chapter, however, the Spirit becomes personal.

In the first section, Jesus declares that as God gave Jesus as the first Paraclete, so he will ask the Father to send another Paraclete. The use of the word *Paraclete* gives some hint as to the function of the Spirit. *Para* in Greek is to be on the side; *kaleo* is to call. A Paraclete is one called to be on the side of another, a defense attorney, an advocate, a helper and supporter. This Paraclete is also the Spirit of truth.

As Jesus once defended his disciples (even when arrested in the garden Jesus first makes sure the disciples are safe), and he was the truth, revealing God to those who would believe, so the Spirit, the Paraclete, will continue these functions of Jesus for his followers. Jesus must leave but the Spirit will remain. The Spirit continues the function of Jesus for all of his followers.

While he lived with his disciples, Jesus took care of them and now he will not leave them alone, as orphans. The Spirit will be the presence of Jesus with his followers forever. They have believed in Jesus and so they already have life, and now they will have the Spirit to be with them forever. The presence of the Spirit will confirm their belief of Jesus' relationship to God the Father and their relationship to God through Jesus. All they have to do is obey his commandments that have been seen in the two great parables of this gospel: the good shepherd—believe in Jesus; the vine and the branches—take care of each other.

In the final section of this chapter, Jesus dwells on the need for love and the power of his Word. Once the Word became flesh, people could see in Jesus the presence of God; in his words they learned about the meaning of God. Listening to the Word of God in Jesus, believing and trusting in him, brings the person into an intimate relationship with God. Father, Son, and Spirit dwell within the person.

The Spirit, the Paraclete, continues the revelation, the unveiling of God to believers. He will instruct them. In John 16:13, the author goes even further: "When the Spirit of truth comes, he will guide you into all truth." Because of the presence of the Spirit, the follower of Jesus needs no one else for guidance and instruction. For this reason, many in the history of Christianity will question the need for any church authority. The Spirit is enough.

Peace is the gift of the Spirit. In Hebrew, *peace* does not mean the cessation of hostilities but the best of everything. Today the word is used in both Hebrew and Arabic as a greeting. The one who wishes peace wishes the person the best of everything: "May you live a long life; may you see your children's children; may all your efforts be successful; may you be on good terms with your neighbors but especially with God." Jesus gives peace through the Spirit. When resurrected, his first and only greeting is peace—twice in this gospel (John 20:19, 21). To be on good terms with God, to receive the gift of peace, to be blessed with the Spirit, the Paraclete, the individual need only believe in Jesus and take care of the brethren.

PREACHER'S PREPARATION

Both Sundays offer the opportunity to speak of the relationship of Jesus and the Spirit. Pentecost has a different approach to the Spirit. There the Spirit reverses the Tower of Babel and overcomes chaos. Here the Spirit remains with the disciples, continues the revelation of God, renders testimony to Jesus, reveals and explains the meaning of Jesus, and leads the follower to all truth.

The Spirit also defends the disciples. He is their bulwark of defense. He gives guidance and peace. When a follower of the Lord faces critical moments in life, St. Ignatius says that if the person is at peace with the decision, then it is the right one. The Spirit gives the individual the guidance needed, and peace is the result even if the decision may appear to be contrary to what others think or believe, even within the Christian community.

The Spirit present to the individual believer assures that person that one is never alone. The follower of the Lord can face any problem, any difficulty, including death, and perhaps especially death, because the Spirit of Jesus remains present. No orphan exists in the Christian community. Also, when members of the community fulfill their calling and take care of each other, then that concern assures the one in need that he or she is never alone. The Spirit remains and works through others for others.

Sixth Sunday of Easter B

John 15:9–17

The Gospel of John knows only one commandment, the commandment of love. While the Synoptic Gospels speak of the love of God and the love of neighbor following the tradition of Deuteronomy and Leviticus, the author of the Fourth Gospel does not tie these two commandments together. Rather, he speaks only of the law of the love of the brethren.

The gospel for Sunday comes from the final words of Jesus at the Last Supper. During the meal, he calls his disciples "friends." They have listened to all he has said about God, and they have responded to Jesus through faith. When he commands them to love one another, he wishes to leave them as his legacy the same joy that he has experienced as one who loved them because God has already loved them.

During this final talk with his followers, Jesus spoke of the new commandment. Often Christians tend to think that love in the New Testament is different from the Old Testament. They tend to think of God in the Old Testament as the God of justice more than the God of love. Such thinking is not accurate. What is new in the preaching of Jesus is not the command of love since this command already exists in the Old Testament. The criteria used in love make the difference. Followers of Jesus are to love one another as Jesus has loved them. They must love one another as God has loved Jesus and as Jesus has loved. He willingly gave his life for his friends.

In some ways, the Johannine Gospel and letters are the most complex of all the literature in the New Testament, because the author always seems to be dealing on different levels at the same time. In other ways, they are the most simple since they always manage to reduce the gospel to its most fundamental elements: faith and love.

Faith in Jesus is the beginning of the Christian life. Without this fundamental personal relationship to Jesus nothing else can make sense. People may continue to live in a complicated society, and even be involved in a rather complicated community called the church, but unless each individual has personal faith, all else has little value.

The love of neighbor has a similar simplicity. The author of John clearly teaches that if Christians love their neighbor, they love God, and without the love of the brethren they have not the love of God. Here, as in the example of faith, the author falls back on what is essential and refuses to lose track in a world that encourages shortsightedness. When an individual believes in Jesus, then he or she loves the brethren as a natural outcome of faith. Then they have fulfilled the law of God. This might be a simplistic approach, but it is also one that emphasizes the essential. In society, love means many things. The love of Jesus, however, that by which Christians measure their love, means the self-sacrificing love for the brethren first.

If the Gospel of John is simplistic in its emphasis on faith and love, it also is most demanding on the meaning of faith and love. The author invites all to turn to Jesus in faith and base every life on him and his gospel. Then, love as he has loved. That alone creates the church and makes sense of human life.

PREACHER'S PREPARATION

The Gospel of John shows the close relationship between faith and love. Faith forces followers of Jesus to become people oriented within the community. The Fourth Gospel often seems to reduce all to faith and love. The homilist might try to join these two ideas together. If people can trust that someone cares for them, then they can care for someone else.

No one can experience a true love of God unless that love is first experienced within the community. Trusting in Jesus, and thus trusting in God, demands an acknowledgment that faith binds believers together with each other because they are already bound together in God.

Seventh Sunday of Easter
A — *John 17:1–11a*
B — *John 17:11b–19*
C — *John 17:20–26*

This final chapter of the farewell discourses culminates in the final words of Jesus to his disciples. Before entering into glory Jesus offers a final and solemn chant. He remains in the world (John 17:13, 19) but already has left (John 17:4, 11, 12, and 18).

Some have compared this farewell of Jesus to that of Jacob in Genesis 49 and the final speech of Moses in Deuteronomy 32. In the ancient world great personages often offered their final thoughts to their family and friends. Here, Jesus sums up his teachings and his ministry.

Although the speech appears only in the Gospel of John, this does not mean that it has no relationship to the Synoptic Gospels. Some ideas in the chapter can also be found in Matthew 11:25–27 and Luke 10:21–22, as well as in the Our Father in both Matthew and Luke.

It also fits the general liturgy of Passover meals filled with long prayers. The references to the "Hour," the bread of life, treason, and the mission of the disciples all fit the historical situation of the Last Supper. Even if the author or inspirer of this gospel arranged the final composition of this prayer, the elements go back to the historical Jesus and the historical Last Supper. Jesus has already passed to eternity, which is made present now as the Johannine community celebrates the Eucharist. The prayer of Jesus has become the prayer of the community.

In the sixteenth century, David Chytraeus, a Lutheran, gave to this chapter the title: "The High Priestly Prayer of Jesus." It is that, but not the prayer directed to the ordained priests of the sacrament of order.

Rather, it is for all who share in the one priesthood of Jesus: the disciples.

The chapter seems to have four divisions:

vv. 1–8: the task to be accomplished and is accomplished

vv. 9–19: the prayer for those who are given to Jesus and whom he makes holy

vv. 20–23: the prayer for future generations

vv. 24–26: the prayer for the day when all will be united in glory

In the first section, Jesus lifts his eyes to heaven. In this gospel, the author has two levels: heaven and Earth. Jesus is in both, but now the glory once in heaven is now on Earth. The hour of glory (and humiliation) has come. The mission is accomplished. God is glorified as the Son is glorified, and this takes place on the cross. Jesus gives eternal life *now*, not in the future. He has made known the Father, has manifested the name. He completes the revelation of the name of God to Moses. Now God will be what God will be: present powerfully to save.

Some have responded and believed. The author returns to the theme of the prologue and the glory promised there that is full of grace and truth, compassion, kindness, mercy, and fidelity. Those who believed share in that glory *now*.

In the second section, Jesus prays for his disciples in relationship to their mission. They too will reflect the glory of God the Father. He is leaving and has left. They need help, and the Father will give them that help. God will make them holy for their mission and guard them because of their union with Jesus. All are in union with God, with Jesus, and with each other. Only one does not belong and he never did belong (1 John 2:19). The disciples must be filled with courage and optimism because of the joy Jesus has already given them. They will accomplish the plan of God because it is God's plan. The Word may bring conflict, but they live in the world as if they did not. They will take their source of strength from the Word of God.

Verse 19 sums up the ministry of Jesus and the meaning of his priesthood. Jesus makes himself holy so that his followers may be holy. By his death he gives glory to God and sanctifies his followers. As holy people, separated from all that is not divine, the disciples will also glorify God. As Jesus manifested God, so his disciples will do likewise by living like God, and showing to others the virtues of God, the same virtues first mentioned in the prologue: compassion, kindness, mercy, and fidelity. Jesus has made all this possible by his death.

In the third section Jesus prays for the church of all times. The unity here on Earth reflects the unity of Father and Son. This demands knowledge of those united but especially the love of those united. The Father, Son, and disciples are all united through the power of the Spirit in every epoch. So united, the followers of Jesus will conquer the world not through violence but through love.

Finally, Jesus declared what he wants: "I would have...." Jesus is not the judge for he has been glorified. Where Jesus is he wants his followers to be and vice versa. They *now* contemplate his glory in faith. The final glorification of Jesus manifested to all creation will include his disciples. He has revealed God, and now his disciples will continue the revelation for they will experience the love of God. In this way they will share in the one priesthood of Jesus. Now Jesus can go to his death in which he reveals his love of God and humanity, and through the resurrection God reveals love for Jesus and ultimately for all humanity.

PREACHER'S PREPARATION

To try to convey the full impact of this chapter even in three homilies would never suffice. Each year the preacher may choose one theme, provided the overriding theme of verse 19 remains in place—even if that particular verse does not appear in every year. "Making holy" is essential to understanding the ministry of Jesus and the ministry of the disciples in the church.

People are holy when they manifest the qualities of God as Jesus did. If the glory of God is the manifestation of God's power and goodness when people live the divine virtues, God's power overcomes all vices and God's goodness preserves life for the believer and thus in the world.

Jesus has given life to his disciples and this life will never end. Eternal life has begun now in the lives of every believer. They have known the love of God, and thus they can show this love to others. Since they know God loves them, they can love one another.

TEXT: The final prayer of Jesus with all of its elements.

CONTEXT OF THE GOSPEL OF JOHN: Sums up the ministry of Jesus: "making holy."

CONTEXT OF CONGREGATION: They are holy even if they commit sins of weakness.

RESPONSE: Choose one of the virtues—compassion, kindness, mercy, or fidelity—and live it at least for today.

Pentecost

John 20:19–23

Without the Spirit of Jesus, there is no church, no community of believers who have made their commitment to the Lord, no guidance, and no unity. With the Spirit, the church has a future. A community of believers gathers and is guided and united by the Spirit, and thus the church is born.

Pentecost celebrates the great sense of belonging that Jesus has accomplished through the gift of his Spirit. People are united in faith and in hope and inspired with the fire of love of God. With the Holy Spirit, people can be the presence of God in the world today.

Pentecost reverses the Tower of Babel. At one point, the Bible narrates that all people were united and could communicate, but sin, evil, and pride had destroyed the unity of the human race, made so evident when people with different languages tried to communicate. The people of the Earth had been dispersed and confused, and thus their unity was destroyed. But now there has been a change. The coming of the Spirit of Jesus has united people. Parthians, Medes, and Elamites, all people who lived in strange lands, could listen and understand. Now the human race was united in a common bond of faith and love. They could communicate with each other because of the presence of the Spirit of Jesus.

This work has avoided reference to any of the texts of the Sunday Masses other than those from the Gospel of John. This Sunday demands an exception. The full understanding of the role of the Spirit can never be exhausted in Christian tradition and thus, historically, the church has expressed in many ways what the presence of the Spirit has meant to the community of faith.

The sequence for Pentecost is a beautiful expression of the depths of the meaning of the Spirit. Jesus has promised and given us his Spirit, and now all can feel the Spirit's effects. The Spirit is Father to all, the giver of gifts, and the light of people's hearts. The Spirit gives relief and rest. The Spirit gently bends what is rigid, warms what is cool, and gives direction to the wayward. With God's Spirit, human salvation is assured for the Spirit gives the gifts that were promised: wisdom, understanding, counsel, knowledge, fortitude, piety, and the knowledge of the Lord. Pentecost is the great feast when the church recalls the origins of the Christian community and pledges anew to be sensitive to the presence of the Spirit today.

The gospel reading presents the gift of the Spirit in the context of peace and forgiveness. The disciples gather for fear of the Jews, but also with great anxiety. They had failed Jesus in his hour of need and now if he is truly risen what will he say to them? What will he expect of them? In the midst of profound human failure, Jesus wishes his disciples the gift of peace. Then he breathes on them and gives to the church the gift of the Spirit and the power to forgive.

On Calvary, Jesus had handed over his Spirit to the two perfect disciples, his mother and the Beloved Disciple. Now he gives this same Spirit to all his disciples along with the gift of peace and the ministry of forgiveness. The birth of the church at Pentecost signifies the great ministry of the whole church: peace to all and forgiveness for all.

The church today, as well as in the world, needs both peace and forgiveness. As the Christian community gathers to recall the past origins of the church, it has the opportunity to pray with great fervor that the Spirit of God will be present and accepted, so that the peace and forgiveness that all need will be the Spirit's most recent gift. On Pentecost, the whole church prays: "Lord send forth your Spirit and renew the face of the earth."

PREACHER'S PREPARATION

Pentecost offers many possible themes for preaching. As the reversal of the Tower of Babel, Pentecost teaches that the Spirit of Jesus can unite all people so that they understand each other. Pentecost as the birth of the church celebrates the ministry of the whole church. The sequence gives the preacher the opportunity to acknowledge what the Catholic Church has accomplished in the past with the hope for greater ministry in the future. The homilist can appeal to the congregants to continue their role in ministry, especially as more and more laity are desperately needed.

The Theme of Unity and Communication

TEXT: The reversal of the Tower of Babel; differences are blessings; peace and forgiveness are gifts of Jesus and the Spirit.

CONTEXT: The Spirit alone can unite disparate people; the origin of the church.

CONTEXT OF THE PEOPLE: the great disunity in society and in the church; anxieties, fears.

RESPONSE: Communication and unity demand listening, paying attention to what people have in common, compromising when necessary, and wishing everyone the best of everything, including peace. The sign of peace symbolizes this commitment outside of the eucharistic celebration.

Trinity Sunday A
John 3:16–18

Nicodemus appears only twice during the cycle of Sunday readings: in the Fourth Sunday of Lent, Year B (John 3: 14–21), and then on the Feast of the Trinity, Year A (John 3:16–18). The principal addition in Lent is the prediction of the passion: "As Moses lifted up the serpent in the desert so must the Son of Man be lifted up," and the additional verses on light and darkness.

All of the readings on Trinity Sunday have some reference to Father, Son, and Spirit. In Cycle A, the first reading refers to God as merciful, gracious, and full of kindness. These same qualities appear frequently in the Gospel of John. They are the divine virtues that Jesus manifested and to which the prologue attested: "Full of grace and truth" (John 1:13).

The second reading from Corinthians contains the usual greeting that begins the Mass: "The grace of our Lord Jesus Christ, the love of God and the fellowship of the Holy Spirit be with you all." But why the reading from John?

This section of the discourse of Jesus with Nicodemus deals with the relationship of Jesus to God, and then the relationship of God and Jesus to people. God loves the world; God has given Jesus to the world. Jesus came not to condemn but to save and give life. The only thing expected from people is faith.

This section from the third chapter does not contain any reference to the Spirit, but earlier the author uses a play on words between wind and spirit, which is the same word in Greek. Neither here nor in Lent does the lectionary include these verses, but they are necessary to understand the whole chapter.

Wind comes and goes. People do not see it, but, rather, its effects. No one knows from where it comes or to where it goes but everyone knows it is real. The same is true for the Spirit. In the Gospel of John, Jesus gives the Spirit, which continues the work of Jesus in his followers.

Throughout this gospel, the author speaks of the unity in God and the unity that includes those who believe. The Christian God is a community of persons and to this community, by the power of the Spirit, Jesus invites people. Where people of faith live, God lives and vice versa. Once inside this community, the person need not fear anything, especially judgment, for that judgment has already taken place when the person comes to the light, comes to faith.

The compassionate, kind, merciful, and faithful God manifested in Jesus now invites believers to share the one life of God, especially by living these same divine qualities. The Christian God wants all to belong to this community.

PREACHER'S PREPARATION

This Sunday could begin with contrasting the Christian God of Father, Son, and Spirit with the understanding of God in Judaism and Islam. Jews profess one God: "Hear, O Israel, the Lord your God is one." Islam professes: "Allah alone is God and Mohammed is his prophet." Christians profess belief in Father, Son, and Holy Spirit.

If God is community, then the Christian community should exemplify on Earth the community that is God. Community demands communication with God and with others. Just as believers should listen to God (and God does speak, especially through the Word of God), so they should listen to each other:

> Be quiet and listen to God: the Word, the preaching, and the promptings of the Holy Spirit.
>
> Be quiet and listen to others (everyone old and young).
>
> One sign of not listening: "Don't you think..." rather than "Do you think...?"

Waiting impatiently for someone to be quiet so you can say what you want to say.

Community on earth reflects the community in heaven and both demand listening.

Trinity Sunday C
John 16:12–15

The Gospel of John does not have a clear church structure as does Matthew's Gospel. The emphasis is on faith in Jesus and love of the brethren. These essential elements of Christianity form the basis for the community. Jesus has the authority in this gospel, and he does not share it with Peter as does the Gospel of Matthew. Moreover, the gospel does not use the word *apostle*. More than any other book of the New Testament, this author prefers to call all disciples. He does use the title "The Twelve," but always in a negative sense (John 6:67–71; 20:24). The only one who shares some authority with Jesus is the Spirit, the Paraclete. In the final chapter, the epilogue, some pastoral authority is given to Peter with certain conditions.

In this reading, the Spirit will guide the disciples to all truth. If a person has the Spirit, then that person needs no other teachers. The Spirit given by Jesus will ensure the followers of Jesus that they have all they need to continue to be disciples.

The Spirit will continue the ministry of Jesus by speaking what the Spirit has heard from God. Just as Jesus revealed what he had learned from God his Father, so the Spirit will do. And by so doing he will give glory to Jesus and thus to God.

Glory in the Bible is always the manifestation of God's goodness and power. The glory is first seen in the Exodus in which the power of God is greater than the power of Pharaoh, and the goodness of God becomes evident by giving a captive people freedom and land. The glory of God becomes evident in the New Testament in the resurrection of Jesus. God has power over death, and the goodness of God will not allow the goodness of Jesus to be destroyed.

The reading has references to Father, Son, and Spirit. They all interact with the sole purpose of continuing to reveal to the disciple the meaning of God. The Christian God involves relationships and differs from the understanding of God in Judaism and in Islam. Neither of these great religions depicts God as a community with interacting dimensions. The Trinity in Christianity sets the model for all human interaction and relationships. Father, Son, and Spirit have a common knowledge and a common purpose that outwardly in creation reflects the inner life of the Trinity.

The second reading from Romans also contains references to the Trinity with the same interaction. Here the effects are felt by all those who follow Jesus. Hope comes from the presence of the Spirit given by Jesus from God bringing peace.

The first reading from Wisdom adds to the Johannine understanding of God by referring to Wisdom. In the Gospel of John, Jesus is incarnate wisdom, leading his followers to understand the order that God has implanted in the universe. By knowing this order (through the presence of the Spirit), the disciple lives a life of faith, hope, and love, bringing happiness now and a future pledge of eternal life begun in the present.

PREACHER'S PREPARATION

Trinity Sunday should concentrate on the Christian understanding of God as community. On this Sunday, the preacher might emphasize the role of the Holy Spirit in giving knowledge and guidance to the disciples. This also might be an opportunity to dwell on the Christian conscience in matters of morality. Since a person has entered into the family of God through faith in Jesus, then the presence of the Spirit will help in making moral decisions.

The Holy Spirit is given to the whole church and not just church leaders. Often, the laity will have insights into living a life of faith that will contribute to the whole church. Trinity involves community, which involves communication, and the laity have their contribution to make within the church because of the presence of the Holy Spirit in them.

Corpus Christi A

John 6:51–58

The Gospel of John has the longest treatment of the Last Supper of all the gospels. Yet, he makes no mention of the Eucharist. The section of chapter 6 that forms the gospel for this Sunday clearly contains eucharistic teaching, but it is placed in the context of the whole chapter on the bread of life. Over the years, many have wondered why the author chose to place eucharistic teaching in this chapter rather than in the chapters on the Last Supper.

Chapter 6 is long and includes the miracle of the feeding, the walking on the sea, the teaching on Moses and manna, and then the famous bread of life discourse by Jesus. Some see the whole chapter as eucharistic teaching, reaching a climax in verses 51–58. A careful reading of the chapter, however, points to a wisdom motif, especially in the bread of life discourse. Jesus is incarnate wisdom giving guidance in living. Admitting the wisdom theme, some have read backward from eucharistic teaching to wisdom teaching. The Eucharist interprets wisdom, since through the celebration of the Eucharist an individual gains the wisdom to live life well. However, perhaps the interpretation goes the other way.

Wisdom involves faith in the one who is giving the guidance. Trust forms the foundation for any acceptance of any teaching. The bread of life first demands trust in the one who is offering the bread. Only then can a person accept what the other person has to say.

By the time the Gospel of John was written, Christians had been celebrating the Eucharist for perhaps sixty years. Like any ritual, even the most devout can take it for granted. People who believe in the presence of Jesus in the breaking of the bread can go through the motions without paying much attention to what the ritual means. Religious people can celebrate a ritual lie, because it is too easy to perform the ritual without meaning.

Probably this normal human experience had become a problem for first-century Christians. The author of the Gospel of John knew too well the human propensity for becoming accustomed to doing a ritual without paying attention to its meaning. For this reason, he took the eucharistic teaching from the Last Supper and placed it in the context of wisdom and faith. No one can celebrate the Eucharist unless the person is first a person of faith. The bread of life in the Eucharist presupposes the bread of life accepted in faith by listening to the teachings of Jesus and then living that faith. Only then can a person come to celebrate the presence of Jesus in the Eucharist.

To avoid a ritual lie, the person coming to the Eucharist must first trust Jesus and his words. Participating in this sacred meal actually brings eternal life, not in the future but in the present. Sharing the body and blood in the sacrament brings a person into an intimate union with Jesus and with God his Father. The Eucharist actually gives eternal life now and union with God through Jesus. The ritual accomplishes what it signifies.

PREACHER'S PREPARATION

For both priest and laity the frequent celebration of the Eucharist can become routine. Ritual lies happen all the time in churches throughout the world. All who participate in the Eucharist must constantly remind themselves what it means. They must pay close attention to the readings, to the homily that is always supposed to join the readings to the Liturgy of the Eucharist. Both Liturgy of the Word and Liturgy of the Eucharist are part of one ritual. The celebration presupposes bringing to the Mass the spiritual sacrifice of a life well-lived in faith. Then, by listening to the Word and celebrating the presence of the Risen Lord in a sacred meal, the person gains the support to continue the spiritual sacrifice. Eucharist first demands faith.

Note: In the Catholic tradition, sacraments are expressions of a reality that is already there. Celebrating the presence of Jesus in the Eucharist presupposes celebrating the presence of Jesus in daily life.

This constitutes the spiritual sacrifice. Believers bring this to the offering of the Eucharist, and take from the celebration the desire to continue to offer the spiritual sacrifice. For this reason, the homily is most important to give assistance, as are the careful readings from the Bible. The eucharistic prayer is never sufficient; together word, homily, and eucharistic prayer constitute at least the possibility of avoiding a ritual lie.

Second Sunday of the Year A
John 1:29–34

John the Baptizer is never called *the Baptizer* or *the Baptist* in the Gospel of John. He is simply called John. He has one function: to point out the Messiah. He fulfills his mission well. Unlike the other gospels, the Gospel of John does not record the baptism of Jesus by John. John calls Jesus the Lamb of God, which might refer to Jesus as being the paschal lamb, since Jesus dies in this gospel at the time the paschal lambs are slaughtered in the Temple for the feast of Passover. If this chronology is correct, Jesus does not celebrate the paschal meal with his disciples as recorded in the other gospels, but as a meal on the night before the paschal meal. The Lamb of God may also refer to the triumphant lamb in the Book of Revelation.

John explains the function of Jesus as the Lamb of God: He will take away the sins of the world. Jesus accomplishes that in his ministry and in his dying. All a person has to do to share in this ministry of Jesus is to believe that God has sent him. Accepting Jesus as the Lamb of God brings the forgiveness of sins.

John recognized his role in the plan of God. John does not pretend to be someone he is not. He tells the truth, and evidently some of the disciples of John left him to follow Jesus. He had fulfilled his destiny and ministry.

John explains further why he recognized Jesus. (Only the Gospel of Luke has the story of Jesus and John being related.) The one (God) who sent John to baptize with water revealed to John the ministry of Jesus: He would baptize not with water but with the Holy Spirit.

The significant words in this passage are: "When you see the Spirit descend and remain on someone…." In the Gospel of John, Jesus has the Spirit and when he dies he communicated his Spirit on the two perfect believers: his mother and the Beloved Disciple (John 19:30). The ministry of Jesus rested on his possession of the Spirit, and when he was dying he made sure the Spirit would continue to be present with his followers.

At the Last Supper, Jesus promised to send the Spirit, the Paraclete, the defense counselor, to his followers and this he accomplished on Calvary. Baptizing in water was not sufficient since effective repentance could be possible only through the power of the Spirit.

Unlike the baptism of Jesus in the other gospels, John himself testifies that Jesus is God's chosen one. In the Synoptics, a voice from heaven makes this declaration. In this gospel, the baptism does not take place. No voice from heaven is heard, but the testimony is the same.

At the time of the writing of this gospel, some people still believed that John was the Messiah. Perhaps to counteract this belief, the author of this gospel downplays the role of John the Baptizer. His only function is to point out the true Messiah and declare that Jesus is the chosen one of God.

PREACHER'S PREPARATION

At the beginning of the year, the preacher might explain the role of John as giving testimony and apply it to the lives of all believers today. The word *martyr* means to give witness. It does not mean to die but to offer testimony. Followers of Jesus offer testimony by how they live their lives. Pointing out Jesus to others becomes the actual ministry of Christians. Even among themselves, Christians can help each other to recognize Jesus within the community, as well as in those who are in need. Blessed Teresa of Calcutta helped even very secular contemporaries to see the face of Jesus in the poor.

John was honest. He told the truth even if this meant he would die for telling it. He never pretended to be someone he was not. God called him to announce someone else and not himself, and so he did. Later in the gospel, the author refers to John as a bright and shining light (John 5:35). Certainly, he manifested his commitment to God by his willingness to speak the truth and to die for what he believed, but in this gospel the bright and shining light pointed out Jesus to others. The followers of the Lord today should do the same by how they live their lives.

Second Sunday of the Year B
John 1:35–42

God calls people to life. Sometimes God comes in the quiet of rest and other times in the busy marketplace of daily living. God comes to people where they live and extends a hand, hoping for the acceptance of an embrace that is always freely given. As life is never meant to be taken for granted, so neither is God's presence in life and the offer of faith to be presumed.

But how can people believe in God unless they hear, and how can they hear unless someone helps? How can people believe unless God gives the gift of faith, and how should people recognize God's presence?

The gospel reading records the voice of Jesus and the call. The voice of Jesus addresses those open to be God's servants, and they respond. To come into contact with Jesus evoked a response for those who heard him, who experienced the power of his personality, and who were attracted to his company. Andrew and the unnamed disciple of John the Baptizer address Jesus as "teacher" and wish to be with him. Jesus invites them to come and see and so they stayed. Andrew, impressed with Jesus, decides to share his enthusiasm with Peter, his brother. Peter also hears the voice of the Lord and, responding, becomes the "rock," the leader of the Twelve who will confirm the faith of the apostles when Jesus is no longer with them.

In this brief section in the opening chapter of the Gospel of John, Jesus is addressed as the Lamb of God, Teacher, and the Messiah. In each instance, someone gives Jesus a title. Each had heard the invitation to faith and accepted the Lord. They recognized him and joyfully accepted discipleship. Faith came immediately with little hesitation. The disciples seem to burst with faith enthusiasm so unlike the manner of depicting the followers of Jesus in the other gospels.

What does it mean to become a disciple of the Lord? Discipleship demands a humble openness to hearing the Lord and then responding. People have to create the environment in which the Word of the Lord can come and be heard. Once heard, which must be a passive as well as an active response, the listener becomes active, allowing the Word to have its effect, changing one's life. An active acceptance characterizes the coming to faith. These early followers listen and learn that Jesus is a teacher, the Lamb of God, the one who fulfills the hopes of Israel, and the Messiah who is the presence of God in human history. This is the first step, the beginning of a vocation in life. The second step involves the more practical living out of this calling, based upon the teaching of Jesus as found in the gospel.

Once individuals have responded to the call of God in Jesus, they also receive the promise of "being with him." The followers of Jesus on Earth did not have an easy path, but they lived with the Lord, which made it joyful. If today people listen to his voice and heed his call, they will experience his fellowship. Believers hear that voice in the church where his followers come to recall his memory and celebrate his presence.

PREACHER'S PREPARATION

The homily might center on vocation in life. All are called to respond to life with each person having a contribution to make. The uniqueness of human life brings the possibility of a unique contribution to life. If individuals listen, they can make their mark on this world, which will make it a better place. Everyone has a vocation, a calling, and each vocation sets a pattern upon which a person lives.

No vocation should be considered superior to another, especially when the calling is lived out in a person's individual life. Some might argue that the vocation to the priesthood or religious life is a higher calling, but this is only in theory, never when concretized in individuals. Responding to one's calling in life is the highest form of vocation for that person, and every vocation demands a perduring commitment.

Second Sunday of the Year C

John 2:1–12

Everyone knows the story of the wedding feast of Cana. Here for the first time the Mother of Jesus appears in this gospel (Mary appears again at the foot of the cross. Only on these two occasions does the author mention the Mother of Jesus and, like the Beloved Disciple, she remains unnamed.) With Jesus and his disciples, the Mother of Jesus attends a wedding feast and inaugurates his ministry.

Just as Luke portrays Mary as kind and compassionate in her visit to Elizabeth, so the author of this gospel also records her compassion. To help the couple to avoid embarrassment, the Mother of Jesus asks her son to do something and he responds.

Over the years, many have tried to downplay the dialogue between Jesus and his mother. The choice of words by Jesus in speaking to his mother does not signify a warm exchange. Several levels of Johannine theology seem to be taking place here.

First, Jesus in this gospel seems to separate himself from his blood relations. The new family of Jesus after the resurrection will be based on faith and not on a bloodline. The Mother of Jesus demonstrates faith even if she does not understand her son. She also remains faithful to the end. Faith always demands the acceptance of the unknown and constitutes the true family of Jesus.

In the messianic times, the Old Testament foretold an abundance of wine. At the marriage feast of Cana, the people had much good wine to drink. Jesus as the Messiah had begun the messianic times with his presence. Those present did not realize what had happened. Even the disciples of Jesus, enjoying themselves, did not foresee where it would all end. The "Hour" begun at Cana would culminate on Calvary.

The man who got married was not the groom nor was the woman who got married the bride. Jesus was the groom who entered into human history as the sign of the kindness, compassion, mercy, and fidelity of God. His mother symbolized all who would believe in him as God's anointed one, even if she did not understand everything.

This gospel calls the great acts of Jesus "signs." The author declares that the miracle at Cana is the first of the signs that Jesus will perform. Throughout the first half of this gospel, the author will refer to other signs: the cure of the official's son (John 5:54); "they saw the signs which he did..." (John 6:2); "for this man performs many signs..." (John 11:47); and the next to last chapter sums up the works of Jesus by referring to signs (John 20:30). Each sign demands faith. The true believer sees through the sign to understand something of Jesus and responds in faith.

The hour of his glory, the crucifixion, has not yet come but it had begun at Cana with a request from his mother. At Cana, Jesus revealed the power and goodness of God, as well as the glory of God that would become evident throughout his ministry. People were in need and Jesus responded to that need. "And his disciples believed in him."

PREACHER'S PREPARATION

The marriage feast of Cana concerns faith without complete understanding. It also points to the crucifixion when the hour of the glory of Jesus will take place. Jesus has begun the messianic times by manifesting his care for people in need. The glory of God in Jesus always involves responding to the ordinary aspects of human life. The Mother of Jesus stands for the church, the bride of the Messiah who lives by faith even if never with compete understanding.

As symbolizing the church, the Mother of Jesus and not "Mary," her proper name, has ties to Jesus because of her faith. The same is true for all followers of Jesus. Faith brings a greater bonding than any blood-line. The future is good with a promise of a superabundance of good wine. Jesus has started the process and now all people need to do is respond in faith.

Seventeenth Sunday of the Year B
John 6:1–15

Most cultures, unlike the American experience, consider bread as the staple food for life. Americans see bread as an addition and often not even necessary. However, provided a person has bread to eat and water to drink, that person can live for another day. Bread and water are often taken for granted, yet they remain so important for life.

In the Old Testament, God provided bread for the Israelites as they wandered in the desert. He also provided them with water. Throughout the Old Testament, the combination of bread and water signifies not just physical food and drink, but also spiritual nourishment. Both are essential for human life.

Each of the gospels records the feeding of the multitude. In fact, the evangelists tell stories about feeding six times (Mark 6:32–44; 8:1–10; Matt 14:13–21; 15:32–39; Luke 9:11–17; John 6:5–13). Each story has its own setting and its own distinctive teaching for the followers of Jesus.

The story in the Gospel of John begins the long chapter on the bread of life. People have followed Jesus and now need food. With the same confidence as Elisha, Jesus commands his disciples to distribute the five barley loaves and the dried fish. The people eat, have their fill, and still some food remains.

Readers and students of the Jesus tradition today try to re-examine the various miracles of Jesus to discover the different possible meanings present in what Jesus does in his ministry. They are not anxious to dismiss the miraculous but, rather, seek to find the miraculous in ordinary life. God surely can intervene in human history if God so wishes. In the history of salvation, however, God intervenes, bringing salvation rather than merely responding to the ordinary needs of daily life. Followers of Jesus should not see miracles as suspending the laws of nature, which God has already established; miracles, rather, are part of the daily experience of believers in Jesus.

Through the power of God, Jesus could have multiplied loaves and fishes (although in no account does the evangelist say that Jesus did), so that the crowd would have something to eat. Such a miracle would have been dramatic but short-lived. Once it had passed, people would probably forget that it had happened and continue to go on living their daily lives. But if Jesus could touch people's hearts so that whatever food they possessed could be shared with all of those present, then the miracle would last. People would have made a decision to be generous with what they had and share with those in need. Long after the miracle had taken place, they would still feel the effects within themselves and might remember to continue to perform such miracles when an opportunity would arise.

No one knows precisely what happened in the ministry of Jesus when he fed the crowds. Did Jesus create food from nothing, or did he touch people's hearts so that they gave to each other whatever they had? Both possibilities exist in the stories in the gospels.

Anyone can read the gospels and marvel at what Jesus accomplished in his brief period of public ministry. The true marvel of Jesus of Nazareth, however, lies in the effect of his teaching on millions of people for almost two thousand years. Miracles are part of the human experience; God has created this world having the possibility of the miraculous, but the marvels will be unleashed only through the lives of good people of faith.

Bread remains the staple of life. People still need bread to survive—the bread on the family table and the bread on the eucharistic table. When Christians receive the bread of the Eucharist, their faith is strengthened so that they can perform the miracles that will help bring bread to the tables of the poor of the world.

PREACHER'S PREPARATION

The homilist might choose to explain the meaning of miracles as above. This would also give the preacher an opportunity to congratulate the members of the congregation on their generosity in the past.

The homilist could also encourage continued efforts to provide for those in need.

If parishes do not have a program responding to those in need, they could begin one, whereby the parishioners give food to the poor throughout the year and not just at Thanksgiving and Christmas. Contributing to a food pantry each Sunday would encourage parishioners to share from their abundance, or to share what they have with those who have less.

Eighteenth Sunday of the Year B
John 6:24–35

The entire sixth chapter of the Gospel of John deals with the bread of life. First, the evangelist narrates the feeding with the loaves. Then the scene changes to the other side of the Sea of Galilee, where people had gathered more to see the miracle worker than to listen to what he has to say. The end of the chapter is clearly eucharistic when the author speaks about his flesh for the life of the world. Many scholars see the eucharistic themes throughout the passage. The feeding with the loaves itself has terminology that was used in the celebration of the Eucharist in the early church, and so even in the beginning readers can detect some of the eucharistic teaching of the evangelist. Another theme, however, that is often overlooked in this chapter is faith in the Lord.

In an Old Testament tradition, Wisdom calls to those who will listen and offers bread and wine. Wisdom invites those who seek to be wise to eat at her table, to accept the search that is necessary to discover Wisdom, and to obtain the goal of that quest. Seeking Wisdom is an ever-demanding quest and a never-ending quest.

For the author of John, Jesus is incarnate wisdom. He expresses in his life and in his teaching the hidden meaning that God has implanted in the universe. Like Wisdom, Jesus invites those who are interested to learn from him, to believe in him, and then they will discover the goal of their hopes and aspirations. They will learn the meaning of life and the order that God has implanted in the universe.

The Father had given Wisdom to creation. Now the Father has sent the Son, hoping that people will turn to him and believe in him, and then they will discover Wisdom. The bread of life that Wisdom offered in the past is now offered by Jesus of Nazareth. The only condition necessary is faith. People must freely come to eat of this bread, believe in Jesus, and then they will know Wisdom.

The bread of life discourse begins with the theme of the Eucharist. Some may wonder why the author has placed his teaching on the Eucharist within the context of Wisdom and faith. The other evangelists presented their teaching on the Eucharist during the Last Supper, but the Fourth Gospel, while having the longest section devoted to the Last Supper, chose not to mention the Eucharist. Instead, the evangelist taught his followers about the meaning of the Eucharist by placing his teaching after a discourse on Wisdom and faith, preceded by the multiplication of the loaves. The author also mentioned that some people were interested in Jesus just because he performed miracles, rather than in what he taught.

For the early church, as is true for all times, some suffered from the temptation to see the Eucharist as another mighty work, a miracle, and fail to see that the miracle depends on something prior. The celebration of the Eucharist demands first a faith in Jesus. The bread of life is not just the Eucharist, but it also includes the faith acceptance of the Lord. Before people can truly celebrate the presence of the Lord in the Eucharist, they must first make the initial faith commitment to Jesus. Only then can they join in the celebration.

Christians can still fail at times to see the close relationship between faith and the Eucharist. Only if they have listened to the teaching of the Lord, made their commitment, and tried to live that commitment can they dare to join in the Eucharist. The great wonder, by which believers experience the presence of the Risen Lord in a sacred meal, means nothing unless it is accepted in faith and becomes an expression of faith. Jesus as Wisdom still calls to eat of his meal: believe in him and celebrate the Eucharist.

PREACHER'S PREPARATION

The homilist might choose to preach on the relationship between faith and the Eucharist. It can be more than just a ritual only if people in faith recognize the presence of the Lord both in the Word and in the sacrament.

The homilist might choose to give examples of a difference in meaning that an object takes on because of its personal value—for example, a book dedicated to a person has greater value than a library of books without a personal reference; a piece of jewelry belonging to a grandmother has a greater value than monetary, and so on. Jesus gives new meaning to bread and wine but only if a person of faith recognizes that meaning.

Nineteenth Sunday of the Year B
John 6:41–51

The Gospel of John often presents Christian beliefs in an unusual way. The gospel was written at the end of the first century after the other three gospels had already been written for the benefit of a Christian community that frequently was more charismatic in character. The members of this community emphasized faith in the Lord and a profound love of the brethren. They believed that Christianity could survive only if it was always founded and built upon these two basic elements of the gospel of Jesus.

As a community, it also emphasized not the future but what had already taken place in the coming of the Lord. They did not look forward to a time when they would be fulfilled in the heavenly kingdom as much as they emphasized what God was doing for them in the present. They did not deny future fulfillment but stressed present blessings.

The other writings of the New Testament were aware of the good things that had happened to those who believed, but also stressed a future reality. Eternal life was the final gift that would come after a person had lived his or her life based on the gospel. Eternal life was the reward for living in faith. The Gospel of John saw eternal life as present *now* because of faith in Jesus (John 17:1).

Sometimes people, even Christians, can be so caught up in the future that they miss the reality of the present. Evidently, the Johannine community wanted to safeguard itself against such a temptation. The future would be the continuation of what had already begun in this life in the present.

In the reading for Sunday, two references emphasize the present. Jesus declares that he who believes has eternal life, and also states that anyone who eats of this bread will live forever. Eternal life is not reserved for some future time, and the true believer need not worry about dying for the follower of Jesus lives forever.

A larger section of this sixth chapter of John deals not with the Eucharist, but with Jesus as the bread of life calling people to faith. Jesus is Wisdom who feeds believers, and when they accept him they are people of faith. Only in the final section of this chapter does the evangelist have definite references to the Eucharist.

In both instances quoted above, Jesus identifies eternal life, or living forever, with faith. In another chapter, Jesus states what eternal life means: "Eternal life is this: to know you, the only true God and him whom you have sent, Jesus Christ" (John 17:3). When an individual believes in Jesus, that person has already received eternal life. Jesus will not reserve this great gift for the future, but bestows it upon those who have made their commitment to him, and thus upon those who have accepted their relationship to God.

The Johannine community stressed faith and love. They knew that many people were concerned, even anxious or afraid of the future. They knew, however, even more strongly that no true believers need fear the future, because they have already made their decision and have moved from the darkness of unbelief into the light of faith. The future holds no surprises for the followers of Jesus, but is only the culmination or the ratification of the present. People who live in faith and love have pulled the future into the present and only await a final consummation of the choices and decisions that they have already lived.

Old men dream dreams and young men see visions, and often both miss the reality of the present. Even today, many Christians worry about the past and are concerned about the future. The Gospel of John reminds everyone that God has already shown love for all. God has given the world Jesus who gives eternal life through faith, *now*. Surely God will not hold back any gift in the future. As believers listen to this gospel they become aware of faith and love, the foundations of Christianity, and remember that God's blessings are for now and not just in the future.

PREACHER'S PREPARATION

The homily might center on Johannine realized eschatology. People often need encouragement for the present. This gospel can offer such encouragement as it stresses what they have already received. The preacher might also emphasize faith and love as the essential elements of Christianity that assure a better future.

"Suffer not and enjoy it later" too often has been part of the preaching of Christianity. The Gospel of John contradicts this. Help people to pay attention to blessings already received and then, even if problems arise, faith and hope help the believer to deal effectively with life's daily concerns.

Twentieth Sunday of the Year B
John 6:51–58

The sixth chapter of John is a compilation of various sources with verses 51b–58 coming from one of the later stages in development. The previous verses treat Jesus as Wisdom with the references to the Eucharist as a secondary theme. Even the verses that do carry the eucharistic overtone are more concerned with an agape-friendship meal, with the verses for this Sunday having reference to the Eucharist proper. What is of particular note is the language chosen by the author of these verses. He no longer speaks of the bread come down from heaven; his choice of words is *flesh* and *blood*. It is also of interest that the author changes the Greek word for body (*soma*) to flesh (*sarx*). He no longer speaks of the body of Christ, but the flesh of Christ.

It may well be that the author intends to teach in strong language that it is necessary for the believer to share in the sacrifice of Jesus if he or she is to live. The Greek word for *flesh* had the connotation of flesh that is offered in sacrifice. When believers die to themselves and share in the sacrifice of Christ, then and only then will they live. When Christians eat his body and drink his blood, they are alive, and this they can do only if they are willing to share in his sacrifice.

The Eucharist is not separated from the daily experience of life. In other New Testament passages, the authors speak of Jesus teaching that "he who loses his life will find it" (Matt 10: 39). The teaching is clear enough, but the actual living is as complicated as any human life. The Eucharist demands that believers first die to themselves before they can share in the sacrifice of Jesus and then share in the eucharistic celebration. Jesus died to himself in his acceptance of the will of God and died to himself in his faithful love of all people, even those who rejected him. If a believer in Jesus today is to die to one's self and share in his life, then that person must acknowledge and accept the daily ups and downs of human living. The sacrifice offered is the spiritual sacrifice of a good life lived based on the teachings of Jesus.

Sacraments are expressions of a reality already present. The follower of Jesus can celebrate the Eucharist only if belief in the Lord Jesus is actually lived in daily life. Recognizing the body and blood of the Lord in the sacred meal demands recognizing the presence of the Lord in others, especially those in any way in need. That spiritual sacrifice the believer brings to the Eucharist and joins it with the perfect sacrifice of the Lord. Not only does the celebration of the Eucharist demand faith, as seen in the earlier verses of this chapter, but it also demands living out the offering of Jesus in daily life. The sharing in the sacred meal in the Eucharist presupposes the sharing in the daily meals of everyday life in which people care for each other. Faith expects the love of the brethren, and then all believers can come together and recognize the presence of Jesus in a sacred meal. They had already recognized his presence among the brethren.

PREACHER'S PREPARATION

The chief theme this Sunday is the Eucharist. An explanation of the text as contained in these notes would be helpful to initiate the homily. A strong appeal to "recognize the body of Christ" would be appropriate with the practical implications of how to offer the spiritual sacrifice of a good life.

The chief purpose of the homily would be to relate the celebration of the Eucharist to the daily experiences of life. One presupposes the other.

Twenty-First Sunday
of the Year B
John 6:60–69

The ability to make personal decisions and to live in freedom in security is a precious gift, particularly appreciated today. Unfortunately, Christians live in a world filled with violations of human rights. Americans have become more aware of how this gift of personal freedom should be guarded and cherished. No force should ever be present in an adult relationship. The same holds true for a relationship with God.

The religious dimension that forms part of human experience must be accepted freely. God insists upon this. God called upon the Jewish people to decide freely: Do they serve the Lord God of Israel or the pagan gods beyond the river? But once they choose to serve the Lord their God, they must abide by God's laws. The initial choice always remains free but, once made, the people who accept the Lord God also accept responsibilities.

In the gospel, Jesus offers freedom to accept him and to follow his teachings or freedom to follow another path. He had spoken of himself as the bread of life, asking for an acceptance in faith, but many of his followers find this to be a hard saying and no longer follow him. Jesus turns to the Twelve and reminds them that since they are free, they must choose or go away. If they decide to stay, his disciples have made a personal choice in freedom. Jesus will not force or coerce. A relationship with him, like that of a relationship to God, must be a free personal decision on the part of the individual.

Peter speaks for the Twelve and decides in favor of following Jesus. Where else can they hope to find eternal life if not in Jesus? Peter does not fully understand the implications of following Jesus and his teaching, but is willing to take a chance because he has already experienced the value in a relationship with Jesus. He decides freely, but not without some anxiety and apprehension, because it seemed good to him to remain with the Lord.

God always treats people with freedom and gives the gift of life with no strings attached. God does not interfere in history, does not thunder from heaven if people fail and turn away. God will not punish human freedom. The gift of life demands that an individual freely choose how he or she will live. Free decision forms part of that gift of life and cannot be taken away. Perhaps at times some might like to have this freedom more restricted. People tend to abuse personal freedom and might welcome some divine restrictions, but God will never take away freedom because of misuse. The possibility of freely choosing God and living according to the commandments is a greater good than trying to determine just what everyone might do. To have the possibility of making a mistake, as well as choosing the good, is better than being determined always to choose the good.

Christianity also must respect freedom. No one must become a Christian, go to church, or live according to the gospel. Each decision is personal and free. Just to grow up with Jesus and his church does not mean that someone has personally chosen to follow the Lord. However, once that decision is made in freedom in favor of Jesus, the individual accepts the responsibility to live the gospel.

Sometimes in the past Roman Catholics gave the impression that religion was not based on a personal decision. To be born a Catholic meant to be a Catholic always, and if a person did not practice the faith, he or she was a "fallen away Catholic." In light of the gospel reading, such ideas may need rethinking. To believe in Jesus and live according to a Roman Catholic Christian tradition demands a continual free acceptance of Jesus and his church. No one needs to remain a Roman Catholic unless that is a free decision. All anyone can do is hope to repeat the words of Peter: "To whom shall we go Lord, you have the words of eternal life."

PREACHER'S PREPARATION

The homily should be based on the sense of freedom. Perhaps it can be directed toward parents, who must allow their children the freedom to live their own lives. Just as God treats us freely, so parents must learn to relinquish their efforts to control the lives of their children as they become young adults.

The homily might also be based on the need to make a perduring commitment to be a Roman Catholic or, perhaps, the homily could center on human rights. Faith is a gift. A German proverb might help: *"Eine gabe ist immer eine aufgabe"*—"A gift is always a responsibility." Notice that it is the same basic word! Once the gift is freely accepted, then the responsibility follows.

Feast of Christ the King B

John 18:33–37

Kings and queens, princes and princesses, still capture the imagination, even if much of what they stand for in fantasies is not real in actuality. Some modern-day kings and queens exist, but they are only shadows of what once was. Perhaps this fantasy, itself left over from long ago, causes the attraction that many Americans maintain for royalty. The kings of fairy tales were young and handsome, and they cared for their people in every way. The king provided for his subjects spiritually, materially, and emotionally, and the people responded with a loving obedience. Surely history had its share of evil kings, but eventually they were destroyed, and once again a good king would bring peace and happiness to everyone.

In the history of Israel, God alone was king. Once they became his people, God provided for them in every way. Even later, when the Jews wanted to imitate other nations by having Saul or David as king, the fundamental understanding was that these earthly kings were only representatives of God the true king. To God alone the people offered a complete loving obedience.

At the time of Jesus, the Jews expected a messiah to come who would also be a king. They looked to God to give them a ruler who would provide for their needs and vindicate them in the eyes of their enemies. But Jesus as the Messiah refused to allow them to make him their king, and offered instead a spiritual kingdom based on the love of God and neighbor, not an earthly kingdom based on power. He never lorded it over his followers but called them friends. Such unexpected conduct from a king, from a person who was in fact the Son of God, might cause us to wonder just why Christians celebrate a feast of Christ the King. If Jesus himself refused to be acclaimed as king, but instead chose to live a lowly life of service for others, why do Catholics end every liturgical year with this feast?

The feast of Christ the King originated in Fascist Italy in a period of extreme nationalism throughout much of Europe. To counteract this false sense of allegiance, the church reminded its members that the one king for all Christians is Jesus and not any political figure, no matter how powerful. To conclude every liturgical year, Christians gather and proclaim their obedience, their loving allegiance to Jesus, the one who provides for them in every way.

However, in the Gospel of John when the people want to make him king, Jesus runs away. He will have nothing to do with an earthly kingdom for his kingdom is not of this world. Jesus remains a true king, but not in the sense of kings in the past. As king, he is closer to the idea of a good shepherd who gives his life for his sheep. When he comes in glory, he will judge not on obedience to him but, rather, on how much his followers have loved each other. Jesus seeks no triumphalism with pomp or displays of power. He calls believers to love without measure and without any sense of seeking self. He preached a gospel that placed mercy and forgiveness above justice and seeking personal justification.

The kingdom of Jesus exists only in the hearts of people who have felt the gentle touch of his hand and experienced the power of his persuasion. This kingdom will last forever for it is based upon love and not upon power. People proclaim him king by personal choice.

PREACHER'S PREPARATION

The homily could concentrate on a personal decision to acknowledge Jesus as king of the human heart committed to bringing about his reign on Earth. Love is the rule of this kingdom. Harmony and balance form the base with an atmosphere of freedom and a wish of peace to all.

People must choose to allow Jesus to reign in their hearts, love one another, and wish each other peace. All of these themes are contained in the Gospel of John.